FRANCE

FRANCE

Text
CLAUDE METTRA

I
NORMANDY / BRITRANY
LOIRE COUNTRY / CENTER

II
POITOU-CHARENTES / LIMOUSIN
AUVERGNE / AQUITAINE
SOUTH-PYRENEES / LANGUEDOC

III
PROVENCE / FRENCH RIVIERA
CORSICA / RHONE-ALPS

IV
BURGUNDY / FRANCHE-COMTÉ
ALSACE / LORRAINE
CHAMPAGNE
NORTH / PICARDY
ÎLE-DE-FRANCE

4-La cité de Saint-Malo

4-The Old Town of Saint-Malo

4-Die Altstadt von Saint-Malo

5/6

5-Cavaliers aux
  environs de Dijon
6-Briançonnais.
  Pêche à la truite
  dans la Clarée

5-Riders near Dijon
6-Trout fishing in the
  Clarée River near
  Briançon

5-Reiter in der
  Umgebung von
  Dijon
6-Briançon.
  Forellenfischfang in
  der Clarée

▶

7-Pyrénées. Pic du
  Midi d'Ossau

7-Pic du Midi
  d'Ossau in the
  Pyrenees

7-Pyrenãen. Midi
  d'Ossau-Spitze

I

NORMANDY
BRITTANY
LOIRE COUNTRY
CENTER

Right up to the heart of the nineteenth century, one finds in cheap commercial literature a figure which is popular above all others, that of Robert the Devil. Distributed under a blue paper cover by the bookstores of Troyes, circulating in thousands of copies and diverse versions in the most remote country-side, the story of this prince who long devoted himself to satanic works and then found the peace and love of God was the privileged guest during evenings spent socializing in thatched cottages. Here is the subject of this primitive melodrama: Hubert, Duke of Normandy, had been married for forty years, but his wife hadn't given him a child. As he was reproaching her for her sterility, she exclaimed: "If I conceive today, I shall abandon the child to the Devil." And that day she conceived. From his birth on, Satan watched over the child. When he was one year old he looked as if he were five, and he made martyrs of his playmates and spread terror everywhere. Later he left his parents' house and joined a band of ruffians who pillaged churches and massacred travelers; he did

harm to nuns and, as a final blow, he slaughtered in the forest a group of hermits who were regarded as saints. It was after the commission of this last crime that the light of God at last fell upon him. After numerous adventures, he was to live a saintly life to the end of his days, in glory and wealth, which are always, the recompense of heroic souls.

Beyond this romantic imagery, for the figure of Robert the Devil to become so deeply engraved in the popular imagination, it probably had to have a remote historical meaning. And, as a matter of fact, what this tumultuous tale expresses is the singular role of Normandy in the beginning of our national history; it's also the image which the French long held of this maritime province which opened our country to the winds of the high seas. When, toward the end of the eleventh century, Queen Mathilda, with her maids of honor, made the embroidery which is known by the name of Bayeux Tapestry, she was rewriting in her fashion the story of Robert the Devil for this serial-novel hero was like a hisyhly colorful symbol of those Dukes of

Normandy who, at the time when the kingdom was formed, appeared as the true founders of feudal France. From Rollo, Viking in search of solid lands, to William the Conqueror, a whole wild and dominating tribe tried their hand at putting our countrDukes of Normandy who, at the time when the kingdom was formed, appeared as the true founders of feudal France. From Rollo, Viking in search of solid lands, to William the Conqueror, a whole wild and dominating tribe tried their hand at putting our country to use. These were men of great courage, but also of great freedom, of that freedom which is born of the sea and of perils. Thus, everywhere they went, slavery disappeared; but they were also enterprising creatures, concrete people who had a taste for bread, meat and strong drinks. Settled on the shores of theEnglishChannel, they weren't long in demonstrating their constructive spirit; they were war chiefs and later would become ardent Crusaders and founders of Mediterranean kingdoms. Having come without women, they easily mixed with the populations of places whose languages, customs and agricultural practices they adopted. From the mixture of races was born the fecundity of that province which for many centuries was the veritable bread-basket of Paris, of that Paris which the Seine brought so close and to which were sent horses, wheat, cattle and cider.

The "Bayeux Tapestry" tells of the Norman epic in England. And this epic thrust is like a spot of light in the anarchical sky of the French lands. In the fusion of powers, the miserable conditions and the spiritual poverty of a people which hadn't yet learned to give a face to its God, the Normans seemed like the promise of a New World. They were youth, turbulençe and faith. Among them appeared the dawn of that Twelfth-Century Renaissance which would cover France with a "white cloak of churches." The Benedictine schools prospered. Vast abbey basilicas rose from the ground, as if after having tested the materiality of that land, after having acquired wealth and greatness there, the men of that country were giving thanks to God in proportion to their will: the Mont Saint-Michel, Jumièges, the Men's Abbey and the Women's Abbey at Caen bear witness to this enterprise calculated in terms of material and labor. It's not at all boldness which takes precedence here, that boldness bordering on madness demonstrated by the builders of Strasbourg or Reims; it's rather a reasonable, pragmatic effort to give the buildings their eternal character.

But this apparent prosaism which lead the Normans far from their soil in search of kingdoms, which transformed the country-side into ploughed land and meadows, which arranged cities so that people could work there and enjoy them, this prosaism has anothersidetoit. Alongsidethefair-eyed gods, there are indeed dark-eyed demons, those which live preferably in Lower Normandy and of which Barbey d'Aurevilly gave the tragic portrait. The novelist of *Les Diaboliques* wrote: "The author of these stories, who believes in the Devil and his influences in the world, is not making fun of all this, and he tells it to pure souls only in order to terrify them of it." But his whole singular work, beyond its supernatural creatures, is the ultimate expression of what could be called the romanesque universe of Normandy, a universe dominated, overwhelmed by men and by viril values, in which all feminine passion seems to be an act of revenge against the order of men. Madame Bovary, the heroines of Maupassant, as well as the companions of the "Bewitched", try desperately to slip their thin and silent existences through the tight web of male certainties. Since men don't give them anything without a price, they have to express themselves, to survive, using only their own weapons: the obscure voices of their flesh and the indistinct memory of their dreams. At the end of their slow, painful road, there are the slow death of melancholy, the hasty death of suicide, satanic spells or the consolations of madness. In the green grass, in the monotony of the marsh, on the banks of a thousand streams whichgoindefinitely towards the sea, prowls a primitive romanticism in which captive woman searches for the echoes of her distress.

It is perhaps this accursed part of the Norman soul which, at the time when Baudelaire was looking for his reflection in poisonous flowers, attracted towards the beaches of the North those who would become the masters of impressionism. In this country devoted to a coherent use of time, here where one feels the weight of long labors and of geneologies,

they discovered the fugitive, the instant which dies at the same moment in which it is born, imperceptible movement which makes of all light and of all life an uninterrupted succession of elusive immobilities. But perhaps what these artists, voluntarily exiled from the Paris studios, found here were the low skies, the misty horizons to which the first conquerors had abandoned themselves when their ships bore them up to the shores of France. Far out at sea, in the foam of the waves and the instability of the clouds, sometimes strange figures take shape: these are phantom ships filled with those ancient Vikings who once ventured upon these shores and who have come looking for their kin. After centuries, in the turbulence of the ports, in the fruitfulness of the labors, in the obstinacy of the tasks, they can still find that bitter taste of life, that somewhat savage joy which, ten centuries ago, announced to a continent ravaged by misery and servitude that a new ferment would restore to the Christian lands the luster of a mythical past.

Normandy was as if swallowed up in France, but the Breton land has enclosed itself in its own space and if, still to day, Brittany seems like a country which no political skill, no economic necessity could dissolve in the national reality, it's because from the beginning she has been charged with a singular mission which, far beyond the French frontiers, concerns the whole European West and the metamorphoses of its lyricism.

Here it is not only a question of the survival of a people which has its language, its traditions, its faith, and which fights with the means at its Sicnocnl ssJninct the clevradation of its disposal against the degradation of its inner life, its liberty, its culture: it is rather a question of the survival, in the midst of a rationalized society, stiffling beneath its innumerable logics, of an imaginative energy which plunges its roots into the farthest reaches of our existence. Brittany is the kingdom of the Imaginary. She alone, with Ireland, represents on our continent that breath of magic which formerly peopled our forests and country-sides with gods, which showed men that, beyond its material servitudes, all life was a witness to another light and that each creature was a portion of a divine creation which never stops being completed.

When Paul Gauguin left the Breton shores to travel to the islands of Polynesia and the heavy-fleshed Maoris, he was not breaking with a familiar world, he was only prolonging, under a sky still virgin, the very dream of which Brittany had been the first habitat. He found again, lost in the faraway oceans, that primitive nostalgia which pushed the ancient Celts to continuously reinvent the world in order to give it a truly divine form. "Who are we? Where do we come from? Where are we going?": these questions to which the painter gave a dramatic representation were those which haunted the Breton heart from the beginning, which are repeated still today, to those who know how to see them, by the land-scapes and the people...

Here, in spite of the grinding material poverty which, throughout centuries, was the daily lot of farmers as well as fisher-men, in spite of the abandonment which was Brittany's share in our national history, that deep disquiet, that mystical thirst of which Christianity is far from revealing all the facets, has remained alive. And at a time when our civiliza-tion, as if worn out by its own conquests, searches desperately in the memory of past cultures or in what remains of primitive societies for spiritual ferments capable of giving it a new impetus, it is possible to find in our own heritage that fertilizing fervor which the Breton epic holds out for us.

This epic, of which practically no literary trace remains, can, of course, be deciphered in everything which for us remains the mark of a long experiment: the rows of menhirs at Carnac, the solitary menhirs of the heath, the small romanesque churches lost in the middle of the forests or the hollow of the valleys, calvaries offering to passersby the image of their heart-break and the crosses or fountains, which are like a sign addressed to wanderers and which all restore, in their fashion, the dialogue of a land and a people. For here, in this country long without a middle class, it's the whole people which expresses in stone its uncertainties and its hopes. But, far beyond the limits of Brittany, it's our whole sensibility which has come to be moulded by the descendents of the Celts, for, as Jean Markale has showed: "The Breton epic can be proud of a numerous posterity, in all periods and all countries. It as had a remarkable fevundity, and that is because the themes around which it is organized are eternal human themes, because the myths which it contains and develops are the essential myths of humanity."

It's not by chance that the principal witness of the only real revolution which we have known since the Renaissance, the romantic revolution, was an authentic child of the Breton sea and land, but in his century Chateaubriand was more a mediator than a creator. Through the myriad resonances of his works, what comes to the fore are the multiple voices of a very ancient qu est, which seem to crys talize in it all the des ires and attractions of a humanity forever fascinated by the need to go further in its understanding of the world. Quest whose charms are revealed to us by the romances of the Round Table, and which corresponds to that thirst, living in the heart of men, to penetrate further into the mystery of life: search for happiness and peace through trials, miracles of the will, confrontations with death; search for the chosen. Woman whose smile gives meaning to man's work and who finds her imperishable embodiment in the figure of Isolde the Blond, creature of fatality, witch and fairy at the same time, who makes of love the incorruptible and moving mirror of real life; but also quest of that other world which is at the same time that of darkness and of light, of that hidden world which the knights of the Holy Grail patiently tracked down and which is at the same time Elsewhere, the great garden of the Absolute and the secret abyss which is deep within each of us. Through this quest, says Jean Markale,

"here is the fantastic which resembles reality, the marvelous which is mixed with the sordid, death which cuts short life and Iife which triumphs over death, the fountain which sets off tempests, wells which overflow and inundate entire cities, birds which turn into marvelous women, lions which speak the language of men, castles which disappear in flames, others which rise up from the deep waters of a sea or lake..."

This great reserve of the Imaginary which is the very spirit of Brittany is equally present on the coasts and in the interior lands. The sea is that open horizon, that sky where the sun and the clouds never stop playing; it is those ports in which the low white houses seem to dream, immobile, before the waves forever beginning anew. It is there that men departed, from the time they emerged from childhood to old age, not to conquer the Ocean but to win its recognition. Peaceful conquerors, wherever their distant fishingspots chanced to take them, they too set out, as formerly the companions of King Arthur, "to the depths of the Unknown, to find something New..." Very often the voyage ended in lands where the human eye is not allowed to look. A simple cross in the cemeteries reminded the living that, at the mercy of a fateful storm, in the void of a hazy dawn, the voyager had perished at sea. Here each one carries his death before him like an armor; absence is also part of the Breton voyage, and that is why the foreigner sometimes has the feeling that an ineradicable sadness lives in these rocks beaten by the wind,

21

these haunted mists, these sandy roads from which one can see the moving hulls of boats. But this sadness is nothing other than the brutal confrontation of the traveler with himself. For the singular charm of the Breton sky, of this apparently deserted land, is that of restoring each person to his own solitude, each being to his own demons.

In order to confront this solitude and to give it its full meaning, the Bretons insert it into their collective life by means of high festivals. The "pardons," beyond their religious celebrations, owe much to ancient magic; there solitary destinies are confounded in a single chant which is the very chant of the earth; and this chant can be found in the solitude of daily life: there are no castles here to bear witness to the world of appearances, but only squires' manors where formerly those noble peasants lived who "went into the fields their sword at their side and, in order to guide the plough, laid their sword down against a stump to be picked up afterwards"; dwellings whose silent humbleness is the very humbleness of domestic objects, of the things of life which are, from generation to generation, the signs of those continuous bonds which bind human existences one to another beyond death.

Here the human order obeys the natural order. It's a secret, subterranean kingdom. And if the memory of death seems to hover over so many places, if the long complaint of men lost in the fatality of their distress seems to rise in the broom or from the groaning of the sea, this funereal presence is in reality an affirma-tion of life. It was in the certainty of their death that Tristan and Isolde, impe-rishable lovers who had known their first embrace and their first sobs in the Breton forest, invented that ardent fire which we call passion and whose burning gives to all sadness its true weight, its unforgettable coloration, its veritable eternity. Through the adventure of this couple, who where supremely happy and yet accursed, who have become the chief model of European sensibility since the twelfth century, what Brittany teaches us is that there is no gap between the world of the dead and the world of the living, between darkness and light, and that every man can, as Celtic mythology maintains, go down into the subterranean spheres and then come back, his eyes dazzled, his heart filled with fabulous dreams, and reinvent indefinitely the changing images of destiny.

If Brittany discovers the reality of the imaginary by interrogating the sky and the subterranean worlds, the Loire countries do not seek at all to take refuge in other universes: for them it is sufficient to give to brute reality the mask of a fairyland, to transform the every-day setting into a theater. Here the light does not prompt men to turn towards their darker side or towards the obscurity of the marine night. On the contrary, it invites them to let the sun, the rain or the stars come to them, in the dormant gentleness which seems to be the musical accompaniment of this happy mixture of water, grass and trees.

These countries, Orléanais, Blésois, Touraine, Anjou, came into History when our kings became politicians more than warriors. In this land, which is as if outside of the great murderous upheavals, they discovered a place propitious both to amusement and meditation. And when Charles VII, who was as yet only the Dauphin Charles, decided to retreat to the south of the Loire in order to let time resolve the national crisis on which his throne depended, it was with the feeling that this happy country was as if naturally excluded from the disorders of war. Moreover, his calculation was not a bad one, for he lived in poverty but in relative sevurity at Bourges or at Chinon until the girl from Lorraine came to take him to Orleans.

When peace came, this Loire region which the sovereigns had considered as a second residence, as a land of refuge where hunts and ladies' games diverted them a while from the servitudes of power, would become the privileged ground of a strange enterprise. The French had discovered Italy, they had wandered, their eyes intoxicated, in this refined civilization in which the princes were artists and the artists princes, and everything seemed constructed, conceived, lived so that men might have the certitude of being, just like the gods, creators of Beauty. Struck by seeing that up to then they had been only barbarians living in discomfort, disorder and melancholy, that melancholy which is illustrated still today by the castle of Loches and its cruel memories, the French tried to create their Italy on the banks of this calm river which was close enough to Paris so that one could enjoy it often, but which was far enough away so that in entering there one had the certainty of entering into another kingdom. It's the only case of complete cultural colonization which can be found in our nation. There wasn't even, at least in the beginning, any imitation, for it was Italian artists who were asked by our sovereigns to make of the Loire country what would later be called the "garden of France": Leonardo da Vinci, the Boccador, Benvenuto Cellini would be the artisans of that architecture, at the same time rational and chimerical, which would multiply those luxurious dwelling in which the concern for pleasure is as great as the taste for appearance.

In the history of French sensibility, the castles of the Renaissance have the same importance as the gothic cathedrals. If the foreigner joins them together in a common fascination, it is because the castles and cathedrals represent an act of faith. What the Loire announced with Amboise, Azayle-Rideau, Chenonceaux and especially Chambord is the advent of man, as Our Lady of Amiens or Saint Cecilia of Albi had announced the advent of God. The poets of the periods, Ronsard first of all but also Du Bellay, had well understood that here was being effectuated a magical transition to another state of man, to a different dialogue between beings and nature. The Valois kings had seen in the Loire country a diversion, a game, a break in the troubled course of life; in reality the Loire was becoming life itself: it was there that words and books took on their true meaning, that the enchantments and rendings of the heart, the only rendings which merit men's attention, found their authentic dimension. These buildings which, merely by the grace of their architectural lay-out, seem to remake the landscape rather than to embrace it, were only an invitation to dream about the infinite powers of our species and about its chances for happiness.

In many respects, this Loire in the Italian style was at first only a decor. Of Italy the French had only seen the appearances, and the castles were theaters where they tried their hand at civilization. They hadn't yet learned that which is the limit of refined cultures, to control their dreams. That is why, under the calcutated arrangement of the architecture, reappears almost always the mask of delirium; it's the revenge of the imagination against the constraints of the mind. It's the festival of words in the face of the silence of contemplation. This French adaptation of the Italian genius is nowhere more dazzling than at Chambord. There, as Michelet rightly remarked, "it is neither the gothic keep, nor the villa, the Italian palace, which has more drawing-rooms than bedrooms, a lot of space with few lodgings. Here society is the essential thing. You really feel it, a curious and restless society. A lot of comfort. Isolated apartments as in a cloister, which do not give access to each other, which are not linked in suites... Outside, the solemn harmony of the towers, with their pinnacles and chimneys in the form of oriental minarets under a majestic central keep. Inside, the diversity, all the ease of movement, the assemblies and the asides, all the liberties of pleasure."

These orderly chimeras, in the midst of this bluish and reassuring horizon, are indeed the works of that triumphant humanism which, in the early years of the sixteenth century, was the cultural habitat of our country. They appear not as a costly distraction, but rather as a challenge into which men threw pell-mell their dreams, their hopes, their fears, their confused passions. Everything here reveals a sort of intense fever, as if the architectural gesture had something as ephemeral, as elusive as the achievement of pleasure. But this very fever, which is not found at Versailles nor in any of the great classical edifices, has a Promethean touch, as if castles, which up to then had been only force, violence and rigor, henceforth embodied that sovereign rhythm, that profound peace, that mysterious profusion which is the lot of divine creation.

This Promethean touch characterizes everything which goes into the Loire's intellectual contribution to our culture, and it can be resumed in three destinies which found here the source of their genius and which, all three, looked at the world with the eyes of a giant, as if they were guided by the desire to sound the depths of the human labyrinth: Rabelais, Descartes, Balzac. Apparently, nothing in common in these three approaches. The grotesque and burlesque merry-making of Pantagruel doesn't resemble that abstract tapestry, woven from solitude and rigorous calculation, which the *Discourse on Method* and the

Metaphysical Meditations constitute. And if Balzac, like Rabelais, tried to stage the human comedy, he did it according to a magical tonality far removed from the laugh of Pantagruel. There is, however, between these three men a common trait: each of them in his fashion was in search of true creation; each one tried to lift the masks and penetrate appearances in order to discover the depths of our condition. Their adventure is an adventure of knowledge, as is, moreover, the whole architectural movement of the Renaissance in these Loire countries, for in the eyes of the sovereigns who erected Chambord or Chenonceaux, to build in the Italian style was an almost magical means of appropriating all the old learning, the ancient culture of Italy. In a certain sense, doesn't Touraine seem like a country devoted to the religion of culture? Wasn't it under this pale sky that the humanists could recognize their privileged climate, their light? The tradition was an ancient one, for it was here that was born what could be called the first work of our literature, at a time when the French still spoke Latin: *The History of the Franks*, by Gregory of Tours.

In the course of the Middle Ages, it was further to the east, at Bourges, that that cultural impulse had manifested itself whith the most brilliance. From the beginning of the twelfth century, when the builders of Notre-Dame of Paris started work here on a cathedral which is one of the most harmonious of all gothic art, the schools of the capital of Berry receveid the many students from southern France and Italy who were en route for Paris or the university towns of the North. Bourges thus became an important trading center, and great was the prosperity of its fairs. It's not by chance that its walls house the unstable fortune of Jacques Cœur, perhaps the first of our great economists.

This culture of the Loire shone with great brilliance at the beginning of the sixteenth century, but was quickly submerged in the political tyranny of the Old Regime. The humanists wanted to be free men, without any direct relationship with the dominant society, "uncommitted", as we would say today, with respect to the immediate problems of the community. These intellectual sovereigns did not long have a place in a monarchy which wanted writers and artists to be, like actors and courtiers, in the service of the State. If there happened to be a free man like Descartes, he had, in order to live his freedom, to go into exile in Sweden or Holland.

Of this passion for knowledge, which doesn't go without some hardchips Balzac has given, in *La peau de chagrin*, an unforgettable picture which is perhaps the most complete expression of the particular genius of the Loire. In the great monologue which opens the novel he exclaims : "I am going to reveal to you in a few words a great mystery of human life. Man exhausts himsellf by two instinctively accomplished acts which dry up the sources of his existence. Two verbs express all the forms taken by theses two causes of death: to want and to be able. Between these two limits of human action, there is another formula which the Wise seize upon, and I owe to it my happiness and longevity. To Want burns us and to Be Able destroys us, but to Know leaves our weak organisation in a perpetual state of calm... My only ambition has been to see. To See, is it not to Know? Or, to Know, is it not intuitively to enjoy?... The word Sage, doesn't it come from Savant? And what is madness, except an excess of wanting or being able ?"

And it is through this page of Balzac that one grasps the very secret of Touraine and Anjou, a certain image of happiness. Oneunderstandswhy,in the search for their final peace, many sovereigns have wanted to be buried under the stone slabs of the abbey of Fontevrault, why the indomitable Richard the Lion-Heart wished that his heart remain forever entrusted to the stones of a church of the abbey, so that the prayers of pilgrims might cleanse him of his crimes.

But before the peace of the tomb, there is the joy of life; before the gloomy rictus of the skeleton, there is smile of the flesh. And here, the quest of the mind is also a quest of the heart. A moving trace of this is found in those peaceful princes of Anjou who, towards the end of the fourteenth century, seem to have had a presentiment of the charms of the Renaissance. A little later, René of Anjou, in the *Livre de Cuer d'Amour espris (Boots of the Heart enflamed with Lose)*, gives an unaccustomed depth to the feeling of love. But much more than by the poetry of the good King René, today we are touched by the admirable

miniatures which illustrate the precious manuscript of the Cuer d'Amour espris. There humble artisans have left the mark of their dreams, of their expectations, of their joys of love. It was at the time when Anjou was delving deeply into the aspects of love that we see the University of Angers peopled with hundreds of foreign students, that we witness, in 1486, what was perhaps the greatest production of the medieval stage with the performance of the "Mystery of the Passion" by the "scientific doctor" Jean Michel. The performance lasted four days, hundreds of teachers and students played a role, and thousands of spectators thronged to the city to participate together in the reconstruction of the adventure of Christ.

This medieval glory of Anjou, this Renaissance splendor of Touraine show us that these Loire countries, much more than a garden, are a theater where every daydream finds a decor in proportion to its temptation. But it's a theater destined for an intimacy in which God and Don Juan feel equally at ease. Chateaubriand, whose Breton origine made him singularly sensitive to the open light of Touraine, the opposite image to the closed transparency of his own country, has underlined this with regard to Chambord, that palace which remains indefinitely as the symbol of a great movement of our civilization, as the focal point where the inventions of the heart and the charms of the intellect come and intermingle. Evoking Rancé's stay in the royal domain in 1670, meditating on the melancholy twilight of his own life, he wrote: "Chambord has only a double staircase, so that you can go up and down without seeing each other: everything there is made for the mysteries of love and war. The edifice blossoms out on each floor; the steps rise accompanied by small grooves, like the steps in the turret of a cathedral. The rocket, in exploding, forms fantastic designs which seem to have fallen down upon the edifice: square or round chimneys embellished with marble fetishes similar to the dolls which I have seen taken from excavations in Athens. From a distance, the edifice is an arabesque; it appears like a woman whose hair has been blown up in the air by the wind; from close up this woman is incorporated into the masonry and changes into towers; then it's Clorinda leaning against some ruins. The caprices of a flighty chisel haven't disappeared; the lightness and dedicacy of the strokes can be seen in the likeness of a dyingamazon. When you penetrate within, the royal lily and the salamander can be seen on the ceilings. If ever Chambord were destroyed, nowhere would we find the first style of the Renaissance, for in Venice it has been overembellished." And Chateaubriand, contemplating in the royal park the image of his own sunset, added: "What gave Chambord its beauty was its abandonment: through the windows I perceived a dry flower-bed, yellow grass, black fields of wheat: reminiscences of the poverty and fidelity of my indigent father-land. When I went by there, there was a brown bird of some size which flew along the Cosson, little unknown river."

This "little unknown river" joins others, all equally unknown, to give the Loire its indolence and its unpredictable moods. The inhabitants of its banks long persisted in trying to make of this river that for which nature seems to have destined all streams: to serve as a bond between men, to provide between countries arteries for broad communication. These efforts weren't all in vain and, up to the appearance of the railroads, men tried to adapt their labors to the capricious rhythms of the water. But these attempts never succeeded in making of the Loire a true opening upon the sea. Thus geography seemed to impose on Touraine and Anjou a retreat towards the inner lands, in fact distant dependencies of the center which was Paris. You have to go all the way to the mouth of the river to feel the presence of the sea. That is why Nantes, much more than a city of the Loire, is a Breton city, which owes little to its hinterland, but which borrows much of its character from the coasts and heaths of Brittany.

However, what made the fortune of Nantes was the happy combination of the dark forces of Brittany, the desire to leave and the love of the unknown, with the white forces of the Loire, the taste for happiness and pleasure, the love of gambling. In the seventeenth and eighteenth centuries, ship-owners and merchants opened France to oceanic adventure. Towards the Americas the winds lead great ships less concerned for legends than for tangible riches. There were born the promises of that greater France which began with the trade in rum and Blacks, which blazed the trail of an empire established in the distant oceans and which was completed in the nineteenth century when, in the footsteps of the Napoleonic epics, the French turned their eyes away from the Ocean and came back to their native Mediterranean.

It all happened then as if in the depths of its subconscious, the French people, following the example of the barbarian invaders of the third and fourth centuries were attracted by the mirage of the south and the solar bursts of the Mediterranean. There can be seen a historical continuity which our time itself seems to confirm: to the west, the north, the east, the history of France is written in terms of defense, refuge, protection. It's to the south that she catches a glimpse of her own transcendence, in nostalgic search of that Mediterranean civilization of which Athens and Rome were the symbolic figures. That is why in the nineteenth century, when Europe was launching into the conquest of new worlds, France, which was then the triple fruit of the Revolution, the Empire and the old monarchy, sent its soldiers, its missionaries and its peasants towards Africa, giving up that Atlantic destiny to which, nevertheless, the western provinces called her.

In this particular attitude of the national consciousness probably lies the relative abandonment in which the French community has left the western regions all throughout the nineteenth century. Neither thc industrial revolution nor the intellectual revolution reached these lands which were thought to be marginal and which became in fact slave territories, only good for providing the streets of Paris with cheap labor. In the eighteenth century, Bretons and people from the Loire, loving liberty and rich in venturesome spirit, went to prospect the coasts of Canada, the islands of the Tropics and the deep seas. In the nineteenth century, they made up the continuously renewed supply of domestic servants, heavy labor and prostitution. The voices, often burning, broken, which are raised still today in these western regions simply express a century-old protest against the neglect in which France has left its Atlantic provinces.

I

NORMANDIE
BRETAGNE
PAYS DE LA LOIRE
CENTRE

NORMANDY
BRITANY
LOIRE COUNTRY
CENTER

NORMANDIE
BRETAGNE
LOIRE-GEBIET
ZENTRUM

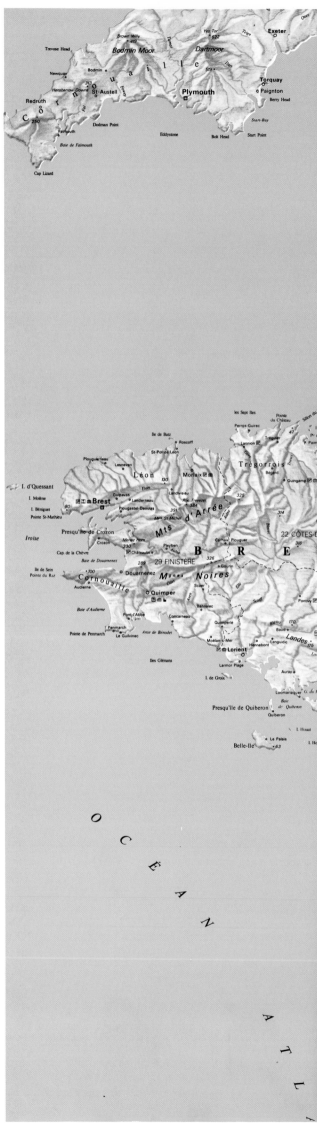

8-Chaumière en Pays d'Auge
8-Cottage in the Pays d'Auge region
8-Strohhütte im Pays d'Auge

9/10

9-Caen. Les maisons de la rue Saint-Pierre
10-Le château d'O

9-Houses in Rue Saint-Pierre in Caen
10-The château d'O

9-Caen. Die Häuser der rue Saint-Pierre
10-Das Schloß von O

11-Les falaises d'Étretat
11-The cliffs of Étretat
11-Die Klippen von Étretat

14-Le Mont-Saint-Michel
14-Mont-Saint-Michel
14-Der Mont-Saint-Michel

17-Belle-Île. Bateaux au Palais

17-Belle-Île. Boats in Palais

17-Belle-Île. Schiffe in Palais

19/20 ▶

19-Piriac. Le port
20-Erquy. Le port

19-The port of Piriac
20-The port of Erquy

19-Piriac. Der Hafen
20-Erquy. Der Hafen

18-Rochers à l'île d'Ouessant

18-Rocks on the island of Ouessant

18-Felsen auf der île d'Ouessant

21/22

21-Quiberon. La côte Sauvage
22-Les aiguilles de Roc'h Trévezel dans les monts d'Arrée

21-Quiberon. The "côte Sauvage"
22-Jagged rocks of Roc'h Trévezel in the Arrée hills

21-Quiberon. 'La côte Sauvage'
22-Die Spitzen von Roch Trévezel in den Hügeln der Arrée

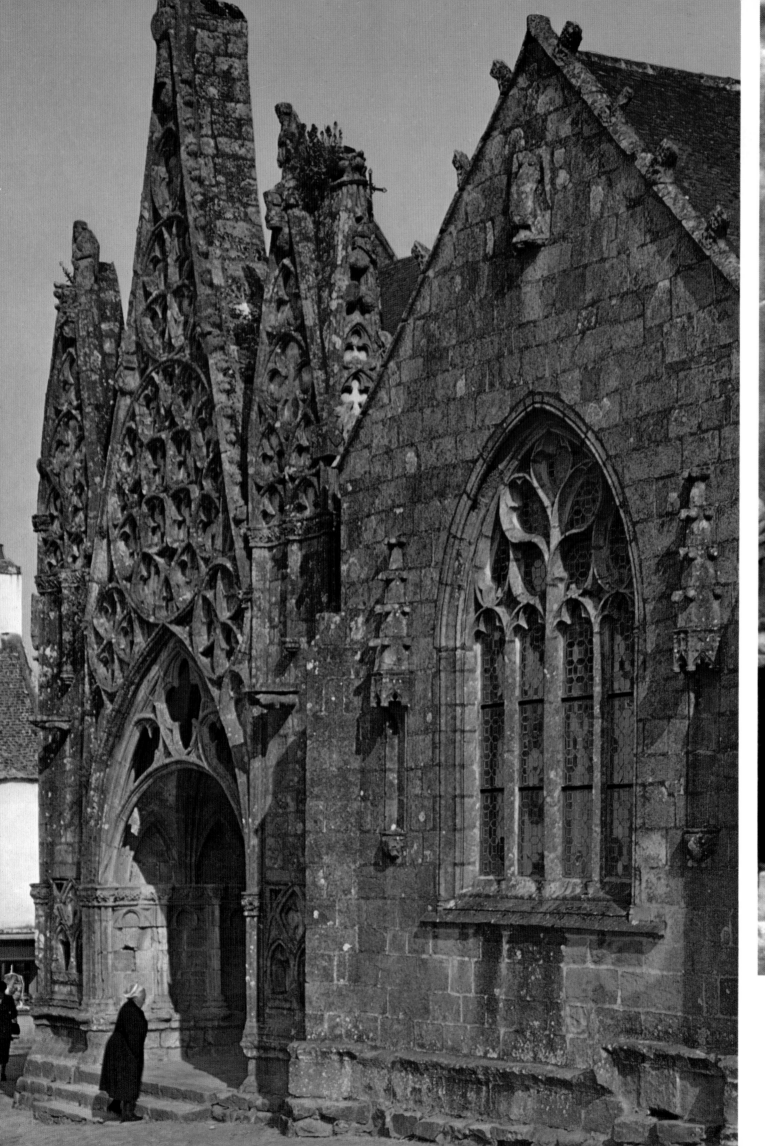

23/24

23-Église de Pont-Croix
24-Calvaire de Saint-Thégonnec

23-The church of Pont-Croix
24-The Cross of Saint Thégonnec

23-Kirche von Pont-Croix
24-Kalvarienberg von Saint-Thégonnec

29-Rochers sur la côte Altlantique

29-Rocks on the Atlantic coast

29-Felsen an der atlantischen Küste

30-Le château d'Ussé
31-Le château d'Azay-
    le-Rideau

30-The château of Ussé
31-The château of
    Azay-le-Rideau

30-Das Schloß von
    Ussé
31-Das Schloß von
    Azay-le-Rideau

34/35

34-Beauregard. La galerie des portraits
35-Amboise

34-Beauregard. The portrait gallery
35-Amboise

34-Beauregard. Die Ahnengalerie
35-Amboise

36-Le château de Chenonceau-sur-le-Cher

36-The château of Chenonceau on the Cher River

36-Das Schloβ von Chenonceau am Cher

37/38 ▶

37-L'escalier François Ier à Blois
38-Chaumont-sur-Loire

37-The staircase of François I in Blois
38-Chaumont-sur-Loire

37-Die Treppe François Ier in Blois
38-Chaumont-sur-Loire

39 | 40
     | 41
     | 42

39-Cheverny. *Intérieur*
40-Saumur. *Le château et le pont
    sur la Loire*
41-*Le château de Meillant*
42-*Le château et la ville de
    Montsoreau*

39-Cheverny. *Interior*
40-Saumur. *The château and the
    bridge over the Loire River*
41-*The château of Meillant*
42-*The château and the city of
    Montsoreau*

39-Cheverny. *Interieur*
40-Saumur. *Das Schloß und die
    Brücke über der Loire*
41-*Das Schloß von Meillant*
42-*Das Schloß und die Stadt von
    Montsoreau*

43-Le château de Chambord
43-The château of Chambord
43-Das Schloß von Chambord

44/45

44-La cathédrale de Bourges
45-L'église de Nohant

44-The cathedral of Bourges
45-The church of Nohant

44-Die Kathedrale von Bourges
45-Die Kirche von Nohant

46/47

46-Une chaumière dans la « Grande Brière »
47-Dans « l'île » de Fedrun

46-A cottage in "Grande Brière"
47-On the "island" of Fedrun

46-Eine Strohhütte in der 'Grande Brière'
47-Auf der 'Insel' von Fedrun

48/49

48-Argenton-sur-Creuse
49-Un étang en Sologne

48-Argenton-sur-Creuse
49-A pond in Sologne

48-Argenton-sur-Creuse
49-Ein Weiher in Sologne

II

POITOU-CHARENTES / LIMOUSIN
AUVERGNE / AQUITAINE
SOUTH-PYRENEES / LANGUEDOC

In his native province, Richelieu, then at the pinnacle of his power, wanted to have his Chambord or his Fontainebleau. On the incertain boundaries of Touraine and Poitou, he had a city constructed which has the rigor and severity of the early classical period. This utopian city symbolized the general aspiration of the century for abstraction, restraint and austere solemnity. This triumph of reason was short-lived: the wealthy lords whom the Cardinal had, with a certain authority, "invited" to build there withdrew immediately upon his death, and the artificial city remained as the sterile sign of an abolished splendor. The question might be asked whether the failure of that concerted city-planning wasn't a result of the country itself. Of course, it was there that René Descartes came into the world and grew up, that great geometer of universal motion and magnificent stage-director of the lights of the mind; but alongside this Cartesian clarity, these western regions display a love of unreason, a penchant for dreams which show that their true destiny belongs to the secret strata of the mind.

Nature itself shows us this. Marshes and woods, fields and forests are not the juxtaposed elements of an unstable geography. Everything belongs to the same mental landscape which, like that of Brittany, is a country inhabited by the gods, but differently. Not far from Richelieu, there is Loudun and its possessed, in whom God, the angels and the Devil speak at the same time. Not far beyond, there is Chinon with that Rabelais who never stops painting the masks of a grotesque world and who rediscovers the tracks of Gargantua, the old Celtic hero. Finally, everywhere there are the legends and the tales told to pass the evenings, but also the superstitions of the common people, and especially that Melusine whose tragic and marvelous story charms the imagination, bestows a feminine grace on nocturnal terrors and reconciles men with serpents.

Melusine was a child of the water whom a noble lord discovered, to his delight, near a fountain and who agreed to marry him on the condition that he swear never to seek to see her on Saturdays and never to observe her in her nakedness. For a long time their union was unclouded, until the day when, overcome with suspicion, the lord followed her to the cellar where she withdrew on Saturdays. There he watched through the keyhole while she took her bath, and he discovered that she was a mermaid. That evening, Melusine left the conjugal bedroom in the form of a serpent, and it is as a serpent that she protects dwellings, and especially the castle of Lusignan, in Poitou, which had been the cradle of her ephemeral happiness. The Emperor Charles V, traveling in the Loire country, came to Lusignan to hear old women tell the piteous tale of the girl with the tail of scales, and Brantôme relates that "some old women said that they sometimes saw Melusine come to the fountain to bathe there, in the form of a very beautiful woman and dressed like a widow; others said that they saw her, but very rarely, and then on Saturdays at vespers, bathing, with half the body of a very beautiful woman and the other half in the form of a serpent. According to such women, she also appeared on the top of the high tower, half woman, half serpent, and they added that whenever some great disaster or death or change of monarch took place in the kingdom, three days before, she could be heard to cry out three times with a shrill and dreadful cry."

This legend is only one version among many of the story of Melusine, and the comparative study undertaken by Jacques Le Goff of all the versions of the myth allows him to demonstrate three primordial functions of the fairy-serpent, which we shall furthermore see emerging later (and this is not without its importance for the witch trials and the revolt of the Vendée royalists) in the cult of the Virgin Mary. Melusine appears first of all as the fairy of the harvest: she ensures the prosperity of the crops and, child of the clearing, defends the fields against the forest. Next she is a fairy builder: she builds castles, abbeys, cathedrals and cities. Finally she is a fertility fairy: she watches over round bellies, protects children from sickness and ensures the multiplication of the tribe.

These three privileges of Melusine correspond rather vividly to the prayers of that people of western France which built Poitiers and La Rochelle, raised up in the most remote country-side that multitude of little churches, certain of which are among the most beautiful which the Middle Ages have left us; this same people, after having redesigned the countryside in order to practice a cultivation corresponding to the requirements of the elements, after having brought into play trees and forests in order to create those woods which are like a garden arranged by a distracted schoolboy, sent a good many of its children in the seventeenth and eighteenth centuries to populate Canada. They brought to America the type of dwelling which remains today that of Canadian farmers and of many farmers of the northern United States.

These voyages towards America demonstrated on the part of the peoples of Poitou and Vendée a love of winds and spaces; there were probably among them many adventurers, pirates or buccaneers whose names have been lost to history, but those hardly went to the northern lands where men's only wealth was courage and endurance. They went rather towards the Equator and the Tropics in quest of perilous treasures borne by chimerical Orients. But, marginal colonists or navigators, they were obeying those same dreams which had formed Melusine and given to Christ and His saints, such as they appear in the frescoes of Saint-Savin, such an engaging familiarity.

Because of that spirit of enterprise which so vividly characterizes the peoples of Vendée and Saintonge, the kings of France founded many hopes on the development of the coastal cities and especially La Rochelle. If Richelieu bitterly defended this city against English ambitions, if against the Protestants he made of it the symbol of the triumph of reasons of State, it is because for him it was the Ocean Gateway, France's opening to the great commerce of the continents. Colbert followed him in this design, and it is perhaps to this love from afar by the great servants of the monarchy that La Rochelle is indebted for being one of the most preciously classical cities in our country.

The taste for wandering is also the lot of the provinces neighboring on Poitou, Limousin and Auvergne, but it's a wandering of a wholly different sort. Here nature, that is to say, the mountains, holds man back. They hold him back by the obstacles to travel which they create, also by the difficulty of every-day life, which requires all the vital forces and leaves little time for dreaming. But they also hold him back through a whole network of mental habits difficult to break. For the mountains are a refuge; they enclose the living in the hollow of a valley, on a steep hill-side which is also a clearing, and there men are, as in a nest, both cut off and protected from unknown horizons. Besides, it is well known how much more than any other country-folk mountain people are attached to their native soil. And the word nostalgia (etymologically, homesickness) was created in the seventeenth century to designate the specific melancholy which took hold of young mountain boys who had rashly enlisted as mercenaries in the armies of princes and who were unable to survive far from their familiar villages. This human store-house which the mountains form, especially along their borders with less elevated lands, explains perhaps why we find so many prehistoric dwelling-places on the edge of the Massif Central. Of course, the hunters of Lascaux found in caves a relatively safe shelter against natural calamities of all sorts, but the caves too were the extreme frontier of their audacity. To live there was to live in proximity to those broken contours where the reference points were convenient, familiar. To go away was to leave the refuge and abandon oneself to those vague horizons where one knew not the gods, the demons and the beasts. Consequently, all the heights which border on the "limagnes" (low, fertile plains of Auvergne) were neolithic fortresses, then Gaulish camps.

After the fall of Rome, as after the collapse of the Carolingian empire, Auvergne, which was situated somewhat outside the great routes of the West, was relatively well protected from the catastrophic turmoil of invasions and migrations. When, with the help of the demographic explosion of the eleventh and twelfth centuries, France awakened to prosperity and invention, this central region represented an appeal, an entreaty; it offered itself to the new spirit. It was a time when pilgrimage routes were multiplying, and Auvergne would represent an exemplary crossroad in this spiritual wandering. Of course, this province is on the direct line which leads from northern and eastern France to the sanctuaries of the Pyrenees and to Saint James of Compostella, but that isn't the essential source of the privileges of Auvergne; there is first of all a fact of a material nature which remains very true today: this country is the perfect place for walking on foot. The extreme diversity of horizons, the multiplicity of relay stations, isolated farms, springs, active towns and — something which counted a lot in gothic times — safe roads, for the robbers and brigands of the highways and byways preferred to establish themselves in proximity to the bridges of the Rhone and the Loire, these are so many factors which favored the anonymous walker set out, like the father of "the young girl Violaine," to meet God, having left his home, his farm, his workshop without asking how many years or decades would go by before he would again cross the threshold of the dwelling of his ancestors.

But the analysts of religious sensibility could add that the very landscapes of Auvergne are marvelously in tune with that ardent meditation on which medieval faith was nourished. And all romanesque or gothic architecture is a reflection of this meditation. Here the sanctuaries are smaller, more intimate than anywhere else. Auvergne isaland of solitary prayers, like Brittany. The churches, and that is probably the stroke of genius of the artists of the period, are in complete agreement with the setting, as if the temple, in the biblical sense of the term, weren't only the building itself, but the entire site. The builders made an extremely subtle use of nature. They probably wanted to show that God isn't enclosed within the walls of the temple, but that he is everywhere, in the abundance of trees, in the song of birds, in the wind which blows the dead leaves. This God is the God of the fields and mountains; it isn't the God of the city who triumphs in Paris, Chartres or Amiens. A profound harmony is established bytheuseofstone whose color corresponds to the general color of the country. This is particularly evident at Conques, but it can also be seen at Le Puy, Issoire and Orcival. From stopping-place to stopping-place, the medieval traveler could have the feeling of never leaving the house of God, for each church was surrounded by a sort of sacred aura which peopled forests and pastures with the divine presence.

By a strange reversal of ancient callings, Auvergne, starting in the Renaissance, would no longer be the destination, but rather the starting point for travel. From the sixteenth century on, the Christian people scarcely visited the distant sanctuaries any more. Saint James of Compostella was now only a ghostly reflection of an exhausted faith. And as if she could not console herself at no longer seeing wanderers beneath her walls, Auvergne took to the road. A relatively unambitious road, and almost always the same: the one which lead masons, carpenters and tacticians to Paris or Lyons. This travel wouldn't stop until the beginning of the twentieth century. In the craftsmen's guilds, those from Auvergne held a not unimportant place, and popular literature offers us many attestations of these often hazardous departures towards the big cities. One of them is particularly instructive: the *Memoirs* of Martin Nadaud, former journeyman mason of the Creuse. At the age of fifteen, this humble peasant left the family farm with his father to work on the construction sites of the capital. This was in 1830, and they had to go to Paris on foot or, when possible, by taking advantage of the kindness of a wagon driver. Here is how Martin Nadaud relates his first nights in the Paris house where the masons from the Creuse found themselves: "In the bedroom there were six beds and twelve lodgers. We were so crowded one on top of the other that there remained only a corridor twenty inches wide to serve as a passageway along the room. I wasn't long, in fact, in becoming acquainted with my companions. Night and morning I heard many conversations from one source or another, one more humorous than the other, always meaningless, when they weren't exasperating or stupefying, for children... The soup in the evening was sometimes served an hour or two before we arrived, depending on the distance we had to cover from the work site to the house." After three or four years, the journeyman would go back to the village; if he found a girl who would have him, he generally got married; the day after the wedding he would go back to Paris to work for three or four years.

This appeal of the big cities which lead the people of Limousin, the Creuse and Auvergne towards Paris or Lyons from the beginning of the sixteenth century on, was hardly felt in the provinces of the South. This area offered its inhabitants sufficient resources so that they didn't wish to go seek their fortune elsewhere. In Aquitaine as in Languedoc, far from Paris, were constituted5 very early, civilizing zones to which History was to give diverse fortunes. The western, Atlantic region, from the Gironde to the Spanish frontier, was for centuries a theater of confrontation between England and France. But here it is not only a question of military confrontations, which were often a settling of scores between mighty lords. The true confrontation was that between the respective geniuses of the French end English peoples. There is a man from this region who, more than any other, symbolizes this division, and that's Montesquieu. To that rational rigor of the French temperament, to that intellectual abstraction prophesied by Descartes and which often encloses the French in struggles of principle in which reality is totally eclipsed, Montesquieu answers with a temptation which seems specifically English: the conquest of happiness. He introduces into the national intelligence a dimension which is too often forgotten, respect for concrete situations, by criticizing all that is specifically theological in the French temperament: excessive belief in ideas, love of discussion — which is only a love of words —, taste for formalism. He endeavors, as do all the English philosophers since the Middle Ages, to consider human society not in terms of God but in terms of man: "The clemency of the government", he wrote, "contributes marvelously to the propagation of the species. All republics are the constant proof of this, and more than any other, Switzerland and Holland, which are the two worst countries in Europe, if you consider the nature of the terrain, and which are nevertheless the most populated... Men are like plants, which never grow favorably if they are not well cultivated: among unfortunate peoples, the Species loses something and sometimes even degenerates. France can provide a fine example of all this. In past wars, the fear which all the children of the family shared of being enlisted in the militia forced them to marry at too tender an age and in the midst of poverty. Of so many marriages were born many children whom we are still looking for in France and which poverty, famine and sickness have carried away."

In reality, what Montesquieu was seeking was a means to help men live together, to refuse the division into parties, factions or sects which has always been the characteristic of the French political genius. It's a debate which we shall encounter again more than a half-century later, in 1792 and 1793, in the conflict opposing the Girondins and the Montagnards. If the Girondins appear then as the defenders of local liberties, the accusers of revolutionary centralization, it's because they remain faithful to a democratic intuition of which Montesquieu, before Tocqueville, was the first prophet and which today inspires the regionalist movements.

The universe of Montesquieu is that of the possible, the real. It is very much in tune with the general spirit of this oceanic shore which has always regarded the horizon as a line to be crossed in order to multiply the chances for human accomplisment. The men of the region were great navigators, but they were peaceful navigators, educators and not missionaries, merchants but not slave traders. It's again Montesquieu who wrote: "There are two sorts of happy people. The ones are keenly exvited by the objects accessible to their soul and which they can easily acquire. They desire keenly, they hope, they enjoy and soon they start desiring all over again. The others have their machine so constructed that it is gently and continuously aroused. It is entertained but not agitated: a reading, a conversation is sufficient to them." It is probably this second form of happiness which the philosopher made his own, it's the one which we find in the great period of Bordeaux, the eighteenth century, at the time when, through the discrete luxury of the private homes, the multiplicity of diversions, the taste for commerce, a way of being and living asserts itself in which the middle class found its justification.

In Montesquieu as in Montaigne a superior wisdom asserts itself, an order which comes from a concerted equilibrium between the intellect and the heart. There can be seen a refusal of the tragic which is one of the most refined aspects of our culture, which Nietzsche praised with fervor in French moralists. And this wisdom is indeed what inspired Henry IV, child of Béarn and mediator between the disasterous tensions which were shattering that great and sensitive organism which was thé French nation. In this Atlantic South crossedby manifold cultural currents, was forged avery special, sometimes very skittish, sense of liberty one which manifests a will to open life up, to maintain constantly open the promises of the future. In the uncertain realms of the heart, that openness which is generosity identically marks the great lyric poets who have found their roots here: between the works of Marguerite de Navarre, Francis Jammes and Maurice Ravel there is at least one point in common, that passionate search for the right tone, for the bare truth, for the inner order.

If these Atlantic regions have obeyed the slow movement of their becoming, patiently seeking their place in the complex play of History, neighboring Languedoc asserted very early a sovereignty of which it has trailed, for eight centuries, the painful nostalgia. For true civilization started here, between Toulouse and the Rhone, at a time when the countries north of the Loire were still steeped in barbary. It is here that in the twelfth century, opposing the tender rendings of passion and sensuality to the warlike furors of feudalism, the fair ladies of the castles invented love and its charms. It is through the myths of passion of the South that the legendary figures of Tristan and Isolde make their way, that fatal love will become the major theme of western poetry.

This Occitanian passion is not a liberation of the senses, a permission. It is the route of an inner experience at the end of which each of the lovers finds his true finality. Its essence is first of all mystical; it leads to the "joy" of love. This joy will become one of the inspiring currents of our sensibility. It is, according to Charles Camproux, "the free exercise of the activities of the whole man, as free as a bird in space without limits. It's a long way from this active joy to the much simpler joy of satiation which is only its normal and merited consequence. It's also a long way from this active joy to the fatal love of the Ancients, which engenders all the consequences of madness, or to that of the romantics, source of melancholy or cause for suicide. This active joy can be easily found in the heart of a Saint Francis of Assisi, who practises it freely in contact with nature and with creatures, in order to raise himself up to divine contemplation; it can be found in the Franciscan conception of salvation, which believes that the direct reading of the book of Nature permits each person to know God."

But the joy of the troubadours, that extasy of the "heart enflamed with love," would die with the Albigensian Crusade and the extermination of Catharism. A whole civilization, which had found in romanesque art its specific expression, was destroyed by a war of conquest which, starting in 1209, would anihilate one after the other its spiritual and material foundations.

However deeply the Occitanian soul was wounded in the Catharist struggle, it is nevertheless continued in that fidelity to its architecture of which we find an example in the admirable constructions of red Languedoc: Toulouse, Albi, Rodez, Cordes, and so many other cities or sanctuaries of brick or sandstone, world of ardent light in which the southern French genius found a mystical flame comparable to that which, a little later, would illuminate Rhenish Christianity or the Flemish spiritualists. Albi remains the incomparable symbol of this bond between the past and the future, for the construction of the cathedral of Saint Cecilia began many years after the last fires were lit for burning Perfects at the stake, and as if in order to give thanks to God for having helped in the destruction of the heresy. But the secrets of the ancient builders continue to animate the pink walls, as if in the moving scale of colors men had tried to restore the deep tonalities of the human being.

In reality, in spite of the execution fires, in spite of the threats, Catharism has never completely died in Occitania. It has remained, on the contrary, the first example of all movements of protest against civil or religious authority which assert themselves from the latter part of the Middle Ages right up to the threshold of the modern era. As the Austrian historian Friedrich Heer writes, "the spirit of the Catharists will survive all the persecutions. With a sure instinct for spiritual affinities, the Huguenots of the sixteenth centuries, so numerous in this part of southern France, will invoke the Catharists and will see in them the representatives of the primitive Church. Bossuet, champion of Catholic conservatism under the reign of the Sun-King, will attack them as the prevursers of the Reformation; he will consider them as members of that Church of the Devil which from century to century carries on the fight against the Church of Rome. The tragedy of the Perfects is inextricably mixed up with that of the whole courtly civilization in its Languedocian bastion; but it is also linked to the fate of all popular religious movements of the thirteenth and fourteenth centuries."

The posterity of the Catharists is, as a matter of fact, in the heretical and revolutionary ideologies which will trouble the religious and political life of Europe in the latter part of the Middle Ages, but it is also in the long struggle which the Protestants of Languedoc, the Cevennes and the Alps will carry on in the seventeenth and eighteenth centuries, struggle which will find its major accent in the war of the Camisards. It all took place as if this Languedocian South had always been, since the gothic period, a continual ferment at work to call into question a French civilization which, in its internal structure, was a heritage of the northern regions of our nation.

Thus many southern intellectuals have been able to describe the history of this region as a tragedy of discord, a drama of cultural exile and material oppression. Of this discord Robert Lafont sees the last expression precisely in that Protestant war which ended in 1710 with a peace of terror, and in which the southern people had risen up against what they considered to be a colonization by the absolute monarchy.

"The revolt of the Camisards", he writes, "is the last of the great confrontations in the Old Regime of the peasants and artisans with the order of the privileged. Consider its leaders : Jean Cavalier, journeyman baker, Gédéon Laporte, artisan; these men are combattants formed by a long misery; their cruelty is in proportion to the repressions which preceded their insurrection and to those which answered it. They stay underground and blend into the rural population which never betrays them. They lead the fight against taxation and never stop repeating it. The motive of faith is a cover for class struggle. Moreover, in this struggle Calvinism loses its rationality; a prophetic hysteria submerges it, bringing back to the surface of history the old magico-sexual heritage of the *Jacquerie* (fourteenth century peasant revolt)."

In reality, this history of Languedoc illustrates in an exemplary fashion the painful and complex alchemy through which a nation is formed, with inevitable confrontations between dominant groups and minorities, with unforeseen acts of vengence which the weakest elements sometimes carry out upon the strongest, with all the resentments and calculations which determine the relations between diverse communities. Apparently, southern France was subjected to the institutions and cultural modes of the northera provinces. The romantic current was almost entirely the work of the northern part of our country. But in the second half of the nineteenth century, in literature, painting and music, it's the Mediterranean element which is predominant, and this cultural emergence is the sign of the ever richer contribution of the South to the national life.

Of course, this existence of Occitania, in which Languedoc holds a dominant place, is far from being written into the institutions and recognized in the facts from which our economic and social life are woven. At least, the weight of the past, that past which can be read with such clarity at Toulouse and Montségur, at Albi and Aigues-Mortes, at Saint-Michelde-Cuxa and the Pont du Gard, gives a voice to a land which long felt itself in exile and which today wants to find again its true being. And to hear this voice, one must not be that hasty traveler who, from one beach to another, from one historic site to another traditionally designated spot, is always afraid that at the end of his trip he will not have accumulated enough memories for the family album. One must penetrate into this strange country as did the pilgrims of the Middle Ages, slowly discover, while coming down from the mountains, the metamorphoses of light and stone, sleep amid the rocks of Saint-Guilhem-le-Désert, dream on the ramparts of La Couvertoirade, city of the Knights Templar, harvest the grapes with the peasants of Minervois, and pray to Sarah or Mary the Egyptian at Saintes Maries-de-la-Mer. For this country of great brightness is a secret country which must be patiently deciphered, in the silence of its men, in the dazzle of its sun, in the peace ot its sleepy villages. It wants to be loved as the ladies celebrated by the troubadours wanted to be loved, with a patience which no waiting could exhaust, with a fidelity which no absence could destroy.

II

POITOU-CHARENTES
LIMOUSIN
AUVERGNE
AQUITAINE
MIDI-PYRÉNÉES
LANGUEDOC

POITOU-CHARENTES
LIMOUSIN
AUVERGNE
AQUITAINE
SOUTH-PYRENEES
LANGUEDOC

POITOU-CHARENTES
LIMOUSIN
AUVERGNE
AQUITANIEN
SÜD-PYRENÄEN
LANGUEDOC

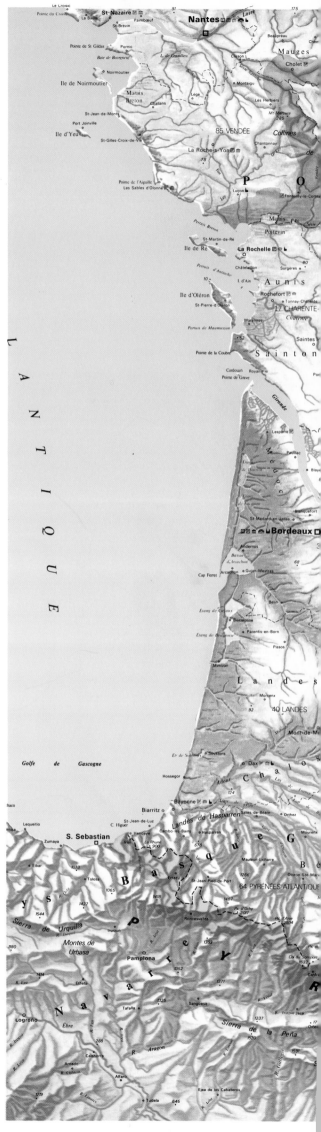

50-Le Quartz au
 Futuroscope de
 Poitiers

50-The Quartz at
 Futuroscope in
 Poitiers

50-Der Quarz am
 Futuroskop von
 Poitiers

56/57

56-Le port de la Rochelle
57-La Dordogne à Beynac

56-The port of La Rochelle
57-The Dordogne River in Beynac

56-Der Hafen von la Rochelle
57-Die Dordogne in Beynac

58/59

58-La Roque-Gageac
59-Pêche au filet en Quercy

58-La Roque-Gageac
59-Net fishing in Quercy

58-La Roque-Gageac
59-Netzfischfang im Quercy

*60-Périgord.
Environs de Sarlat
61-Château de la
Treyne sur la
Dordogne*

*60-Perigord. The
countryside
around Sarlat
61-The château de la
Treyne on the
Dordogne River*

*60-Périgord.
Umgebung von
Sarlat
61-Das Schloß de la
Treyne über der
Dordogne*

62/63

62-Collonges-la-Rouge en Corrèze
63-Le château du Val

62-Collonges-la Rouge in Corrèze
63-The château du Val

62-Coullonges-la-Rouge in der Corrèze
63-Das Schloß du Val

64/65

64-Environs de Murat
65-La chaîne des Puys

64-The countryside near Murat
65-The Puys mountain range.

64-Umgebung von Murat
65-Die Bergkette der Puys

66/67

66-Godivelle
67-Le lac Pavin

66-Godivelle
67-Lake Pavin

66-Godivelle
67-Der Pavin-See

68/69

68-Le château d'Anjony
69-Les orgues de Bort

68-The château d'Anjony
69-Rock formation called "Les Orgues de Bort"

68-Das Schloß von Anjony
69-Felsenformation, genannt 'Les Orgues de Bort'

70-Cloître de la cathédrale du Puy
71-L'église d'Orcival

70-Cloister of the cathedral of Le Puy
71-The church of Orcival

70-Kloster der Kathedrale von Puy
71-Die Kirche von Orcival

72/73/74/75

72-La Majesté d'or de Sainte-Foy de Conques
73-L'église des Jacobins à Toulouse
74-Le château de Cordès
75-Albi

72-The Golden Majesty of Saint Foy of Conques
73-The church of the Jacobins in Toulouse
74-The château of Cordès
75-Albi

72-La Majesté d'or de Sainte-Foy von Conques
73-Die Jakobinerkirche in Toulouse
74-Das Schloß von Cordès
75-Albi

79-Le port de Saint-Jean-de-Luz
80-Saint-Jean-Pied-de-Port
81-Attelage de bœufs

79-The port of Saint-Jean-de-Luz
80-Saint-Jean-Pied-de-Port
81-A yoke of oxen

79-Der Hafen von Saint-Jean-de-Luz
80-Saint-Jean-Pied-de-Port
81-Ochsengespann

82-Chaîne des
  Pyrénées

82-The Pyrenees
  mountain range

82-Pyrenäenkette

93/94

93-Les Corbières. Cucugnan
94-La tour des Cathares à Minerve

93-Les Corbières. Cucugnan
94-The Cathar Tower in Minerve

93-Les Corbières. Cucugnan
94-Der Katharenturm in Minerve

95-La cité de Carcassonne

95-The walled city of Carcassonne

95-Die Altstadt von Carcassonne

96/97 ▶

96-Le pont du Gard
97-Le jardin de la Fontaine à Nîmes

96-Pont du Gard (aqueduct/bridge)
97-The fountain gardens in Nîmes

96-Le pont du Gard
97-Der Garten de la Fontaine in Nîmes

98/99

98-La Grande-Motte
99-L'étang de Thau

98-La Grande-Motte
99-Lake Thau

98-La Grande-Motte
99-L'Étang de Thau

▶

100-Collioure

100-Collioure

100-Collioure

III

PROVENCE
FRENCH RIVIERA
CORSICA
RHONE - ALPS

The Rhone is the Royal Road of our History. This enormous, wils river has always been, for the men who reached its banks, fascination and terror, and in this dialogue of fear and desire is inscribed a civilizing impulse which, more than in any other place, resembles love. The Rhone has not been, like the Seine and the Loire, a bond between the countries which border on it. It has long been a barrier with which men have sought to come to terms. Sometimes looking for its way through steep gorges, sometimes spreading out broadly in the valley and periodically submerging vast lands with its muddy waters, it offered in reality little chance for human implantation. But, long trail of light rending the landscape like a strange scar, it was also a mirror in which men found the reflection of their existence, wild, tumultuous, full of heavy passions. That is why, being unable to settle right on the banks of the river, the ancient tribes established themselves in the immediate foot-hills. Thus, the Rhone would, like the Rhine, be bordered by forteresses, "burgs," whose walls would write the history of this part of southern France, with its confused rivalries between feudal lords, its Saracen or Norman invasions, its religious wars. Fortresses or cities surrounded by solid ramparts bear witness to the distant bitterness of military confrontations. Beaucaire, Tarascon, Villeneuve-lès-Avignon, Roquemaure, Viviers, Châteaubourg, Tournons were so many lairs for observing the roads and, incidentally, raiding merchant caravans.

It is probable that these high places, which still today so forcefully arrest the gaze, were the privileged habitat of neolithic populations occupied with clearing the land and acclimatizing crops. As a matter of fact, they formed the refuges of all those peasants who, often far from the river, whose excesses were always to be feared, were looking for sufficiently irrigated lands. Two peoples, during the Gaulish period, seem to have been particularly hard-working; both of them lived relatively far-removed from the river, since Die, to the north of the Drôme, and Vaison, in the Vaucluse, were their capitals. Further south, Carpentras was the city of the Tricastini.

It was through the sea that the Rhone emerged from the mists of legend. Aroùnd the seventh century B.C., the whole Provençal coast was inscribed in what the mythical geography of the Greeks called the paths of Hercules. Colonists from the port of Phocaea in Asia Minor founded Marseilles and made of it an active trading station. Southern Gaul was thus opened to the combined influences of the Hellenes and the Etruscans. Nothing remains in Marseilles of the ancient Phocean city, but it is possible to reconstruct the lay-out of that checker-board city, with its vast structures housing local crafts, its market places, its agora, its theater and temples to the great godess of Ephesus, under whose protection Ionian colonization was placed.

This hellenic center immediately exerted a powerful attraction on the indigenous populations which, up to then, had been little inclined towards the sea. An attraction both material and spiritual, through which the Gauls were transformed in the most natural fashion into Hellenes; and by a slow contagion, this Celto-Ligurian civilization penetrated to the heart of the Rhone valley. "The Phoceans", would later write a historian of the time of Augustus "whose ancestors descended from the Vovontii of Vaison, tempered the barbary of the Gauls and taught them a more pleasant life. They taught them to cultivate the earth and to surround their cities with ramparts. Such was the progress, at that time, of men and of things that it seemed, not that Greece had gone to Gaul, but that Gaul itself had been transported to Greece." And it's on this Greek model that the fortifications of Baux and Perredon were erected towards the third century, that Entremont and Roquepertuse were constructed. The statuary of this period illustrates the happy fusion of the indigenous mythology with the Greco-Etruscan mythologies. One of the themes most often treated in the friezes of the sanctuaries or in the stone figurines is that of the realm of shadows, of that otherworld in which heroes find immortality; there appears the demon who refuses the dead entry into the lands of light, and it is this same demon that we shall find much later in medieval statuary, at Digne, at Saint-Gilles, at Saintes-Maries-de-la-Mer, at Arles especially, in the dramatic depiction of the Last Judgement.

Thus, when the Romans made of Provence the penetration route towards Gallia Narbonensis and Spain, they found there an active center of civilization which would peacefully open itself up to conquest and become a mirror of the imperial splendor. This adaptation of Roman civilization to Provence reveals to what extent, from the second century on, this region possessed an original substratum and spiritual experience. It is Roman art which appears here, but profoundly transformed by the double heritage of the Celtic tribes and of Greece. As a matter of fact, it is marked by a religiosity far removed from the ritualistic formalism of Rome, as if the continental gods and the primitive gods of the eastern Mediterranean had joined together here to form a particular image of man, nature and life.

There was in the Romanized Provençal civilization a Dionysian touch to which the theaters especially bear witness. Much more so than the circus games, whose blossoming would coincide with the slow collapse of the Empire, these theaters housed festivals which were collective celebrations in which a whole people found its identity, its direction. If this period can be considered the golden age of Provence, it isn't because it was fecundated by Rome, but rather because Rome came at that precise moment when, through a mysterious chemistry of the earth, of races and of encounters, Provence had reached that historical maturity which gives a country the revelation of its power. There are many countries which do not take part is this fulfillment, either because the elements of this chemistry have destroyed one another, or because the events of History have been too violent, too harsh not to crush the heritage of the past. Our northern provinces, for example, have been the object of too many convulsions to preserve their being in the face of the neighboring countries; and Burgundy offers the example of a province which lived, especially in the fifteenth century, a too full history which, in a way, submerged it. In Provence, on the contrary, the mixture of cultures was accomplished with exceptional harmony. It is curious to see how Roman conquerors, who in the second and first centuries were essentially solidiers, found themselves as if obliged to act peacefully

there, found themselves at last in a universe which was that of the work of daily life, of dialogue. It was later, when Provence had long since found its secret equilibriu,m, that the Romans came back to their conquering vocation in order, with Ceasar, to seize the rest of Gaul.

That light which was Provence's between the second and first centuries is without any doubt that which, still today, gives this land its indecipherable secret. Petrarch at the fountains of Vaucluse saw in them the reflection of a divine creation which was the very image of Paradise. He would rediscover there the ancient gods which have continued to inspire men's lives. It was at that moment that the art of building, which is also the art of living, found its final form. But these buildings weren't the public baths, the mausoleums, the triumphal arches; they were rather, always inscribed in the blue of the sky and the brown of the earth, those villages ever beginning anew, those small towns at the summit of the heights, those farms clinging to the hill-sides. "The world is our home", and "our home is the world": such are the obvious facts which inhabit the inside of these stone structures, a bit transformed in the course of centuries but which, for the most part, haven't suffered any deterioration.

With the Roman colonization began the historic split of Provence. Up to then the privileged shore of a Mediterranean which was itself a kingdom, it would see its destiny set in two directions: western Provence would merge with the Rhone valley, triumphal road of civilization. From Lyons to the South, the river seemed to attract active forces to itself; it would crystalize in its eddies the confused passions of men. Beyond, to the east, coastal and inner Provence would live outside the upheavals of the centuries. Pushed back upon itself, enclosed in its silent life, it was forced to find within itself reasons for living and surviving. And the miracle is this: under the sign of poverty, in the humble servitude of the labors and days, these Provençal peasants pursued their dialogue with eternity. Christianity would take root in these mountains where supernatural powers had kept all their enchantments; far from silencing their voices, it would give them an additional resonance; and even in the heart of the twentieth century, when the solitude of each of these villages has been broken, is not the charm of inner Provence born first of all from the obscure presence of the spirits which inhabit the stones? Fot here everything, beyond the humans, is charged with meaning.

But before we decipher the appearance of these spaces, which remained for yet some time our "Far West", which, in our eyes, can be charged with the same nostalgia as the "Prairie" for the Americans of the end of the nineteenth century, it is towards the Rhone, that great mediator of history, that we must turn our gaze. At the extreme south, the Camargue and the Crau are the lands of wind: there, the basins and their animal profusion; here, pebbles and, fomerly the only property, sheep which still go up in the spring to the pastures of the Drôme. In these two regions, man was a prey to animals, and it was from them that the derived his ancient nobility, his freedom. Wild freedom of raisers of horses or bulls; slow and mute freedom of the guiders of flocks. Countries which are built flush with the horizon, which must be discovered step by step, cautiously, as if here men were only ephemeral guests, tolerated only through the tenderness or indifference of the beasts.

The true human city begins beyond, with Arles, then with Avignon. There, right to the foot of the plateaus, history relates the labor of men: the long effort to adapt to the land itself, which is capricious and difficult, here the domain of vines and fruit, a land of vineyards, olive-trees and vegetable gardens. Human works have been an often cruel game with the water, stone, wind and sun. These four elements make their presence felt with primitive excess, and daily life is an ever uncertain anwer to their chimeras. In the face of them, the people have taken on the obstinate dryness of the landscape, the hardness of flint, the sharpness of the wind, the color of fire. Under the apparent mildness of the days, their existence was long a challenge, the same challenge which the inhabitants of its banks had been forever opposing to the tumults of the Rhone. There is thus here, at the bottom of men's hearts, a kind of dull passion, for it is only through long and difficult love that the land has consented to become human land, to give to the peasants the ransom of their pains.

Nothing has been given here except beauty. It was necessary to acquire by invention and labor that supplementary grace which is like the scar that our species traces on a territory which it wants to make its own. Avignon is the most eloquent witness to this will to be. For the installation of the popes in this city was not the work of chance. Between the conquering, imaginative North, its eyes turned towards the future, and a Mediterranean dozing in its antique glory, cultivating with melancholy the flowers of desire and pleasure, a meeting place in that medieval Europe, uncertain of its future, was necessary. Avignon was the privileged spot of these two hostile energies, both fortress and palace, both house of God and dwelling of forgotten divinities. The popes assembled the phantoms of the whole continent, and there is no city in France which is more Shakespearian. The city and its buildings above the Rhone are an answer to the inexorable mechanism of History, that mechanism which Jan Kott deciphers in the English dramatist: "The natural order violated, in which evil gives birth to evil, where each injustice calls for an avenger, where each crime provokes the following crime...; or yet the impetuous beating of the human heart which the intellect can neither accelerate nor brake, but which a piece of steel cuts through, interrupts once and for all. The black and impenetrable night of History from which the dawn cannot be seen, or else darkness which has invaded the human soul."

For the Palace of the Popes was a rejection of the disorders of the centuries, a fabulous attempt to arrest time, suspend the horror and the confusion of seasons in order to reinvent tenderness and communion. Undertaking which would be short-lived, of which remain only legends and deserted buildings. In its effort to unite the North and South, Avignon encountered only disavowal and silence, that same painful silence which inhabits the mysterious Pietà by the anonymous artist with the broken heart whom we call the Master of Avignon.

When Gaul had been entirely absorbed into the Roman Empire, the city of Arles, western limit of the lands of Provence, appeared as the symbol of that fecund fusion of North and South. Because the dead bore witness to the persistence and virtue of the tribe, the Gauls on both banks of the Rhone chose it to be their necropolis, for nowhere they thought, could the souls of the departed find a better rest than in the Elysian Fields of that city, which is today the Alyscamps. And right up to the twelfth century, so they say, the inhabitants of the river banks, from well above Valence, put their dead in barrels along with some money and entrusted them to the tumultuous waters. At Arles they were carefully retrieved.

The funereal vocation of this mediating place between Languedoc and Provence restores for us the image of what the Mediterranean coast was for along time: a country of ruins. Certain of these ruinsarethemostastonishing vestiges which Roman civilization has left on our soil: Orange, Vaison, Glanum show sufficiently well the civilizing effect of this crossroad of the Empire. Much more than grandeur, what stands out here is a certain art of living. There were all the ostentation and all the imagination of

Rome, but whitout that pestilence of corruptionofthegreatmetropolis. The fall of the Empire anihilated both the material prosperity and the spiritual brilliance of that Provence which was like a double of legendary Attica.

Since that somber night into which the Roman dream collapsed, Provence seems to have been endlessly in search of that lost happiness. Land of invasions, thoroughfare, during the entire early Middle Ages it was a prey to depopulation and violence. When in the eleventh and twelfth centuries, en route for the Crusades, the men of the North discovered the desperate beauty of the Provençal landscape, they did not dream that the true Orient, with its chimeras, its inner gold, was there before their eyes. They continued on their way, wasting their fortunes and their labors, in pursuit of ephemeral kingdoms... Thus, for centuries this country of light would be condemned to retiring within itself, without even receiving some reflection from the blossoming of Italy, although it was so close by.

It was in this isolation that Provence would invent its own civilization. Here the sea counts for little; troubled by the barbarianlike tribes which populate the African coasts, the Mediterranean was no longer that great road of commerce which had put the old lands of Asia and the farthest regions of Europe in touch with each other. If navigation was nevertheless pursued, bringing the rich cargoes of the Orient to the continent, it was Venice which provided most of the traffic. Later, with the discovery of the New World, it was Seville, then the other Spanish ports, which would take over from Venice. When at the end of the fifteenth century France, in quest of adventure, tired of its murderous defeats by England or the Germanic countries, would look to the South for new myths, new spaces to nourish both her imagination and the pleasures of her daily life, she would set out towards Italy, towards the mists of Lombardy or the pestilential misery of Naples, without dreaming that within the kingdom itself existed the chances for its imagination and pleasure. Given over to its solitude, turned more towards the interior than towards the expanse of the sea Provence tried to give a historic meaning to its experience. Placed outside the great trade circuits, prisoner of a land in which pebbles take up more space than silt, she built herself in terms of her poverty. She perched her villages on the sides or summits of hills, as if to better assert her attachment to the soil; here, physically and psychically, men take on a mask of stone, settle into a sort of eternity.

Today when one traverses inner Provence, one remains struck by the extraordinary solidity of the human landscape. There is, in the very arrangement of the villages, in the design which the cities impose on the horizon, in the very situation of the isolated farm houses, something which escapes time, as if the labor of men, their thoughts, their dreams, were accomplished almost subterraneanly, in a universe where the haste of ordinary gestures has lost its meaning. But it is in this suspended time that the human relation finds its particular accent: this people, which is said to be loquacious, is a people of silence. If it carries on dialogue, it is with the trees,the beasts,the sky. The moreone advances towards the interior,towards the mountains, there where the play of light and shadows becomes sharper and more fantastic, the more the dialogue between beingsandcreationdeepens. It goes so far that it is sometimes like a barrier between men, for the solitude of the mountains, adding to the historical solitude of the region, makes every man a stranger. Against this strangeness, however, the inner region was for a long time partially protected by a phenomenon which has nowhere its equivalent: transhumance. Of course, in other mountainous countries herds of cattle and sheep go from one valley to another or, in the course of the summer months, reach higher and higher ground. But here the migration was of another scope: from the Rhone regions up to the high Alps, on dusty roads, climbed vast animal gathering whose tripwasattached to a whole set of traditions of which the traces remain alive today. This phenomenon of civilization, which expresses a constant of very long duration, has not yet been described in its infinite richness. It would probably enlighten us greatly on the most secret part of the Provençal soul.

Inner Provence would scarcely come out of its solitary march until the seventeenth century. Moreover, at the time of Louis XIV the cultural influence of a city like Aix-en-Provence remained isolated.

It was in the eighteenth century, under the influence of the physiocrat administrators, that the region regained, little by little, a share in prosperity. All down through the obscure centuries, an everyday art of life had be constructed which, at the moment Provence opened up to the outside world, became very much in evidence; an art which derived from the humblest things and events: the dwelling, the food, the love of children, the special role of women, the fascination of old age and a certain idea of death. This constant presence of life in death, of death in life is the true bond which unites inner Provence: the plateaus of the Vaucluse and the mountains of Nice, maritime Provence and the Provence of the Rhone. The man who has best captured the particular nature of this solar world, who has been able to read both its sun of fire, which burns hearts and fields, and its black sun, which peoples the imagination with fantastic creatures, is Paul Cézanne, the eternal adolescent of Aix-en-Provence. Three paintings resume his itinerary: *Les Joueurs de cartes (The Card Players)*, *La Montagne Sainte-Victoire (The Sainte-Victoire Mountains)* and *Les Grandes Baigneuses (The Large Bathing Women)*, and each of these paintings is like an inventory of the inner themes of Provençal man. The *Joueurs de Cartes* are every-day coziness, the rough and difficult exchange with the nourishing earth; it's the glass of wine which gives life its savor and freshness; it's the glance, both friendly and distant, full of cunning and complicity, cast on friends, companions of joy, labor and patience.

The *Montagne Sainte-Victoire* is naked stone and lighta all the unknown of Heaven and Hell; but it's the immutable order of the gods and the elements, the secret and logical rigor of creation, and that great architecture of ideas which gives its chances and its abysses to the adventure of the mind. As for the *Grandes Baigneuses*, it's the lunar transposition of the great subterranean disorders of dreams and nightmares; it's the joyful tenderness of the flesh in the great springtime of a refound paradise; it's the call towards the vast spaces of the sky and sea mixed; there, the women, matrices of human hope, are a blue vault supporting all the weight and all the warmth of the world. Through these three depictions by Cézanne, what stands out is the very truth of the Provençal landscape: the truly human land which gives men light and a desire to be, rather than a desire to possess.

*
* *

It was necessary to await the middle of the twentieth century and the great seasonal migrations towards the sun and the beaches for the French to discover Corsica. For the long-distance travelers of the eighteenth and nineteenth centuries, Italy was too rich, offered too many attractions to curious minds and senses, for them to turn towards these burned mountains over which hung strange legends. Moreover, the shadow of Napoleon somewhat obscured the historical relation of the island with the continent. Imperial grandeur had been

Corsica's gift to France, but it was an ephemeral blaze; the storm having passed, the island came back to its silence and its ambiguous folklore of the vendetta, bandits of honor and weeping women.

Today, a new life is offered to Corsica. The independence of North Africa has made it the nation's farthest frontier in the Mediterranean. The economic and social transformations of the continent offer it chances which History has always denied it: that of the tourist trade, first of all, then those which are born from men's labor. These chances derive especially from the breaking of the very ancient solitude which, if it were prolonged, would threaten to turn the island into a vast reservation, a melancholy land of refuge, condemned to a vegetative existence. Today, thanks to the multiplicity of exchanges, the mingling of men and of goods, Corsica is in a position to relive the experience of Languedoc and Provence, to invent its personal share in a Mediterranean civilization which, under new guises, continues the historic effort of three thousand years.

Since the end of the Middle Ages, life had withdrawn little by little from the southern part of the Rhone. Of course, the fairs of Beaucaire and Tarascon helped to attract merchants and vagabonds, but the true movement had been shifted to the north, and it is Lyons which, since the Renaissance has become the major city of the Rhone valley. If the Loire is the poetry of the Renaissance, Lyons is its prose. It was there that men deployed

144

with an exceptional success, the economic imagination and material intelligence of that sixteenth century which was the dawn of the contemporary world. At this crossroad, which during the Empire had been the capital city of the Gauls, bankers and merchants multiplied those enterprises which would be the foundation of modern capitalism. But these men of commerce were also men of culture: it is here that the true birth certificate of the book in our country can be issued. At that time, tlhe editors and printers of Lyons could rival the great masters of Basel or Nuremberg, and later of Amsterdam. All the roads of France converged towards the fairs of Lyons, whose fortune has remained intact, and thanks to them, by way of Venice and the great Lombard cities, the products of the Near East reached our country. This hard-working tradition of Lyons would be confirmed in other fields, justifying in advance what would become the central idea of the merchant class in the Europe of the Enlightenment: work has as its just recompense ease and perhaps luxury. Of this luxury, silk was the symbol; that silk which would adorn the heroines of refined passions, and which was the magnificent and useless gift of Lyons to aristocratic Europe. The pleasures of the mind with books, the pleasures of the body with fine clothing, the pleasures of power with money, Lyons, in the wake of its prosperity, would also be the capital of eating and drinking. From neighboring Bresse, from nearby Beaujolais, came those meats and wines which are also, if

one is to believe Rabelais, the characteristic of man.

This brilliance didn't go without disorder, and the misery of the silk workers in the eighteenth and nineteenth centuries reminds us that silk is the luxury of some and the distress of others. Modern distress which hardly resembles the fundamental poverty of those interior lands beyond the Rhone which, from Geneva to the Mediterranean and under very different aspects, unites the people of the mountains and plateaus, all those peasants of Provence, Dauphiné and Savoy for whom existence is an incessant struggle against the elements, whose ruses seem to be renewed periodically by the Devil. In the north as in the south, if one is to believe the legends, it is the realm of the Great Fear. Here man is naked against the sun, the snow and the night. It is from his terrifying solitude that he must derive both hope and subsistence.

*
* *

That humanization of the landscape which characterizes Provence is not at all the case of that Alpine continent which was for a long time outside French civilization. Here, geographic terms do not easily account for the human reality. The two Alpine provinces, Savoy and Dauphiné, include, both of them, two aspects: there are the mountains, their deliriums and their servitudes; there is also that long succession of plateaus, valleys and hills which unites the Alpine massifs with the Rhone valley. Thus, from Geneva to Avignon, there follows a series of countries, with various landscapes and resources, which have been constantly mixed up in the history of the Rhone, which have been reached by the same civilizing currents and which have lived from their exchanges with the cities and men of the river.

The mountains have only participated from afar in the experiments of the Rhone country. Here they were rigorous barriers between two worlds, and they would remain that right up to the nineteenth century. Nothing is more surprising today than to read the travel accounts of the romantic era: there the Alps are described in epic tones which well express the kind of terror which men foreign to these lands felt in the face of these eternal snows, these inaccessible rocks. Before they could become a part of history, the mountains had to become a part of mythology, and this they did precisely by means by means of the romantic sensibility. Several myths are intermingled here, which announce the entry of the mountains into the field of our imagination and which remain active in our contemporary sensibility. There is first of all that discovery of nature prophesied by Rousseau, who was himself well taught in the realities of the mountains and who lead writers, artists and later people from high society to set out in search of wild, deserted, barely accessible places. But in the wake of the great exotic narratives of the eighteenth century, this taste for distant nature was turned more toward the maritime expanses, as if the sea were the only true

barrier between man and his kind, between man and his past. Robinson Crusoe was always a man of the islands. In reality, the move to unfamiliar surroundings is always a move towards the Tropics. If there is an action which us repugnant to the human heart, it is that of the cold, and for the man of the ninettenth century, the mountain was ice. It was necessary to somehow melt this symbolic ice, to hide it behind some element evoking inner warmth, for the mountain to take on a human appearance. And this was, by means of romantic lyricism, the invention of purity. A mythology of snow then blossomed which would not have many literary repercussions in France, but which would nevertheless leave its mark on French sensibility through the many "travels in Switzerland" which came into being starting with the Revolution and which were in great favor right to the beginning of the twentieth century. As a matter of fact, the discovery of the French mountains is in part a reflection of the discovery of the Swiss cantons; it isn't by chance. At the end of the eighteenth century, Switzerland became a land of asylym for the numerous political refugees for whom the Revolution had made it uncomfortable to stay in France. It was there that they discovered the snow, the altitude, the happy solitude of the great summits. It was also there that they thought they were seeing the last vestiges of an archaic population which had been protected from the disasters of civilization by the rough virtues of the mountains. Purity of nature and purity of humanity were blended into a single white image, that of the sparkling snow in the blue of space.

To this mythology of nature and purity we should also add, for the end of the last century, the imagery of health. That was the period when tuberculosis, which took so many romantic young women to their graves, found its habitat, and almost its spiritual justification, on the airy slopes of the mountains. That regenerative power of the Alpine slopes would be a determining factor in the passion for the mountains which would bring life, summer and winter, to valleys long buried in glittering silence.

To these paths of the imagination is added a Promethean will to conquer the elements, to confront those dead forms so obviously hostile to human exploration. Today, this Promethean concern takes more complex forms, for it is no longer a question of conquering nature, but of saving it, of partially restoring it to the ancient wildness which was for so long its lot, so that beasts, plants and rocks might retrain that peace which a sometimes thoughtless penetration of human enterprise exposes to an erosion not described up to now in the geology manuals.

Strange reversal of History... Regions long confined to obscurity, countries without legends or memories, returned suddenly to the most ancient memory of our tribe. The whole landscape was charged with a heavy archeological past. We had been content up to then to protect the works of men; now we protect what was before us, what will survive after the disappearance of our species. Men enlarge to the dimensions of creation their own historical experience, taking over responsibility for the totality of that profusion which surrounds us. Through the Alps and the efforts made today to preserve that state of nature which is so deeply affected in almost all countries, have men understood that they were not alone in nature? Have they, as Claude Levi-Strauss says, seized in this new vision of the mountains, "that chance, vital for life, to become detached, and which consists, during the brief intervals when our species can bear to interrupt its bee-hive activity, in grasping the essence of what it was and continues to be, on this side of thought and beyond society: in the contemplation of a mineral more beautiful than all our works, in the perfume, more learned than our books, inhaled in the cup of a lily, or in the wink, made heavy with patience, serenity and reciprocal pardon, which an involuntary understanding sometimes allows us to exchange with a cat"?

III

PROVENCE
CÔTE D'AZUR
CORSE
RHÔNE-ALPES

PROVENCE
FRENCH RIVIERA
CORSICA
RHONE-ALPS

PROVENCE
CÔTE D'AZUR
KORSICA
RHONE-ALPEN

NORD
Lille ■

Amiens ■

Rouen ■
BASSE- ■ Caen   HAUTE-
NORMANDIE

PICARDIE

Metz ■
Strasbourg ■

Châlons-
sur-Marne ■

LORRAINE

RÉGION
PARISIENNE
■ Paris

CHAMPAGNE

ALSACE

BRETAGNE

Rennes ■

Orléans ■

PAYS DE LA LOIRE
CENTRE

FRANCHE-
COMTÉ

Dijon ■

Nantes ■

Besançon ■

BOURGOGNE

Poitiers ■

POITOU-
CHARENTES   Limoges ■

Clermont-
Ferrand ■

Lyon ■

LIMOUSIN

RHONE-ALPES

AUVERGNE

■ Bordeaux

AQUITAINE

MIDI-PYRÉNÉES

Montpellier ■

Toulouse ■

PROVENCE-
COTE D'AZUR

Marseille ■

LANGUEDOC

CORSE

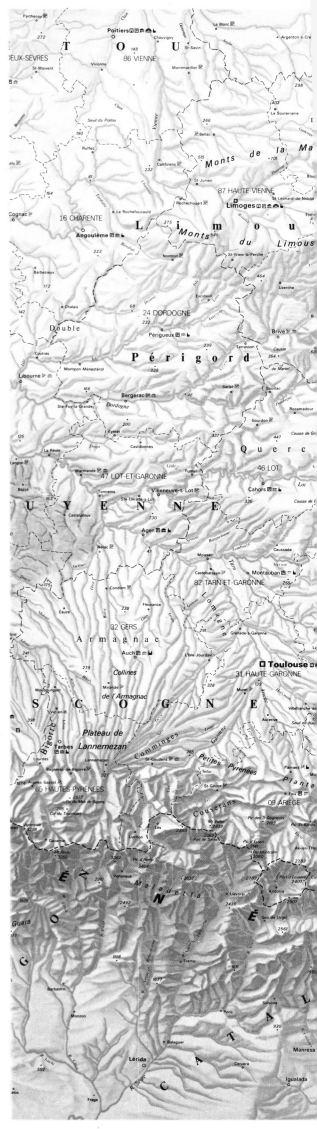

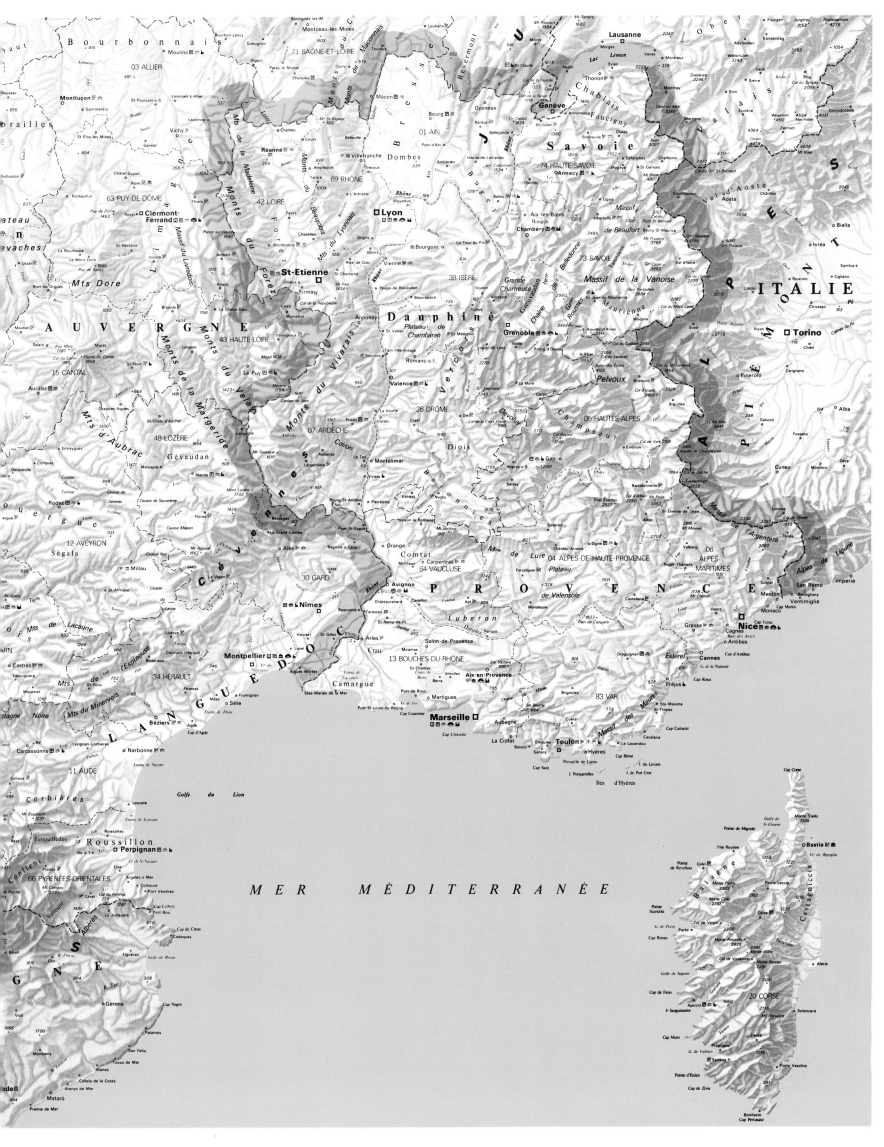

$$\frac{101 \mid \frac{102}{103}}{104}$$

101-Le cloître Saint-Trophisme à Arles
102-Les remparts d'Aigues-Mortes
103-Le château de Vauvernargues
104-L'abbaye de Fontfroide

101-The cloister of Saint-Trophisme in Arles
102-The ramparts of Aigues-Mortes
103-The château of Vauvernargues
104-The abbey of Fontfroide

101-Das Kloster Saint-Trophisme in Arles
102-Die Schutzmauem von Aigues-Mortes
103-Das Schloß von Vauvernargues
104-Die Abtei von Fontfroide

105/106

105-Oliviers à Frigoulet
106-Manade en Camargue

105-Olive trees in Frigoulet
106-Bulls in the Camargue region

105-Oelbäume in Frigoulet
106-Herde in der Camargue

107/108

107-Printemps en Provence
108-Le village des Baux

107-Springtime in Provence
108-The village of Les Baux

107-Frühling in der Provence
108-Das Dorf des Eaux

109/110

109-La fontaine d'Argent à Aix-en-Provence
110-Saint-Antoine de Siga

109-The Silver Fountain in Aix-en-Provence
110-Saint-Antoine de Siga

109-Die Silberquelle von Aix-en-Provence
110-Saint-Antoine de Siga

111/112

111-La ville de Marseille
112-Le cap Ferrat

111-The city of Marseille
112-Cape Ferrat

111-Die Stadt Marseille
112-Das Kap Ferrat

113/114

113-La corniche de l'Ésterel
114-Le village de Peillon

113-The corniche of Esterel
114-The village of Peillon

113-Das Karnies des Ésterel
114-Das Dorf von Peillon

115/116/117

115-Le Vieux Port à Nice
116-L'église Saint-Michel à Menton
117-Dans l'île de Porquerolles

115-The Old Port in Nice
116-The church of Saint-Michel in Menton
117-On the island of Porquerolles

115-Der Alte Hafen in Nizza
116-Die Kirche Saint-Michel in Menton
117-Auf der Insel von Porquerolles

122/123

124-Le fort de Calvi
124-The fort of Calvi
124-Die Festung von Calvi

125/126

125-l'Ardèche à Pont-d'Arc
126-L'aven d'Orgnac

125-The Ardèche River at Pont-d'Arc
126-The swallowhole of Orgnac

125-Die Ardèche in Pont-d'Arc
126-Der Naturschacht von Orgnac

127-Le vieux Lyon
127-The old quarter of Lyon
127-Das alte Lyon

128-Vue sur le Suc de Sara
129-La place Bellecour à Lyon
130-Le tombeau de Marguerite d'Autriche à Brou

128-View of the Suc de Sara
129-Bellecour Square in Lyon
130-The tomb of Marguerite of Austria in Brou

128-Sicht auf den Suc de Sara
129-Der Platz Bellecour in Lyon
130-Das Grab der Marguerite von Oesterreich in Brou

131-La Grande Chartreuse

131-La Grande Chartreuse

131-La Grande Chartreuse

132-Le pic de Bure en Dévoluy

132-The Bure peak in Dévoluy

132-Die Spitze von Bure im Dévoluy

133/134

135-L'église de
    Berland en
    Savoie
136-Chalet près du
    Grand-Bornand

135-The church of
    Berland in
    Savoie
136-A chalet near
    Grand-Bornand

135-Die Kirche von
    Berland im
    Savoyen
136-Chalet bei
    Grand-Bornand

137/138

137-Mazot à Courchevel
138-Le Chatelard en Tarentaise

137-Mazot in Courchevel
138-Le Chatelard in Tarentaise

137-Mazot in Courchevel
138-Le Chatelard in der
    Tarentaise

139-Le lac Blanc au-dessus de Chamonix

139-Lake Blanc above Chamonix

139-Der Weisse See oberhalb Chamonix

140 | 141 / 142 ▶

140-Les Houches et la chaîne des Aiguilles
141-Combloux
142-Le lac d'Annecy

140-Les Houches and the Aiguilles mountain range
141-Combloux
142-Lake Annecy

140-Les Houches und die Kette der Aiguilles
141-Combloux
142-Der See von Annecy

143/144/145/146

143-Le tramway du Mont-Blanc
144-Sports d'hiver aux Contamines
145-Parapente au Mont-Blanc
146-La mer de Glace

143-The Mont-Blanc tramway
144-Winter sports in Contamines
145-Paragliding near Mont-Blanc
146-The Sea of Ice (La Mer de Glace)

143-Die Bergbahn des Mont-Blanc
144-Wintersport in den Contamines
145-Hängegleiter am Mont-Blanc
146-Das Eismeer

147/148

147-Départ vers la vallée Blanche
148-Ski de fond

147-Departure for Vallée Blanche
148-Cross country skiing

147-Aufbruch zum Weißen Tal
148-Langlauf

▶

149-L'aiguille du Chardonnet

149-The peak of Chardonnet

149-Die Spitze von Chardonnet

IV

BURGUNDY / FRANCHE-COMTÉ ALSACE / LORRAINE / CHAMPAGNE NORTH / PICARDY ÎLE-DE-FRANCE

In 1130, Pope Innocent II consecrated at Cluny the largest church in Christendom. All we have left of it are drawings, for it was swept away in the tempest of the Revolution and destroyed at the beginning of the nineteenth century. The construction site, which was opened at the beginning of the twelfth century, can be compared to those of the Pyramids or of the great Iranian cities. All the artisans and architects of the Occident had come to work there; it was they who would carry the lessons of Cluny over the whole territory of France. From there would be born all the great romanesque abbeys: Morienval, Font-froide, Elne, Le Thoronet..., through which the Cistercian movement would shape Christendom. Burgundy then became the center of inspiration of a continent seeking to come out of barbary, desirous of creating between God and man a true city.

As a matter of fact, this creative impulse which then animated the Saône valley was a story of ever-recurring cycles. For a very long time these lands had been a privileged cradle of civilization. Lyons,

which was very close by, had been the Romans' relay station in Gaul. And the Burgundians, who gave their name to the country, having settled on both sides of the Jura in the fourth and fifth centuries, seemed to have become immediately possessed (as one is possessed by the Devil) by the centuries of experience which they found here. The Roman experience, of course, but beyond the Romans, the experience of the Celto-Ligurians, peaceful farmers who, from the third to the first millenium, had given to the landscape the humanized structure which it has kept right up to today and which aerial photography now reveals to us in all its subtle complexity. For from that distant periode dates the present configuration of the country-side, the dialogue of fields, crops, forests, the situation of villages, the lay-out of roads calculated so that men and horses might walk on them. This countryside, of which Burgundy and Franche-Comté offer us the exemplary image, has been slowly designed by the mute complicity of men, wild beasts and trees. "Each of our local boundaries", wrote the great

197

Burgundian historian Gaston Roupnel, "is essentially a cultivated clearing and its limits are the edge of the woods and forests... The original edge is not a brutal gash cut with an axe in a homogeneous mass. It is not the direct, irritated line of contact between two foreign domains with opposing traits and invading energies. Indeed, the cultivated soil throws ceaselessly and agressively back to its borders the couch-grass and brambles; for its part, the forest, in continuous riot against human works, presses upon the cultivated ground a thicket of bushes and a jumble of thorns."

*
* *

For, throughout those centuries preceding History, a singular exchange was established between men, solidly anchored on their land, and nature, which was both a nourishing womb and the forbidden territory of the first human communities. The Roman colonization, on these rigorously worked soils, had only increased their prosperity and sevurity. When, after the year 1000, that vhich was no longer Gaul and barely France again found its creative vocation, the former Burgundian conquerors, intimately mixed with the old Celtic populations, were the first to give a meaning to the Christian adventure. Two major places already drew the frontiers of Burgundy: in the south, Autun and Cluny; in the north, Vézelay. It was between these two sanctuaries that, throughout the Middle Ages, an incomparable manufacturing activity would be manifested, finding its

final embodiment in the brilliance of the Duchy of Burgundy in the fifteenth century, at the time when the history of the Occident was changing directions, when Christendom was dying to make room for Europe.

Burgundy was the privileged ground of that rupture and that metamorphosis. Heir to the culture of both the North and South, fecundated by the Flemish genius, her gaze turned towards those provinces of the South which were streaming with the light of the Rhone, she gave to the works of peace what France and England gave to the works of war. Dijon became, as would later become the proud cities of Flanders, a model and a school. In a century in which Christian faith was dissolving in the fevers of dances of death and of carnivals, the Dukes of Burgundy, rather than constructing cathedrals and abbeys, reinvented houses of men. Mythical house, with its ostentatious spectacles, its funeral rites, its gallery of heroes. Thus, the charter-house of Champmol rose from the earth, necropolis of the Dukes where Claus Sluter sculpted his "Well of Moses", which would be copied throughout Europe so that glory might be given to recumbent figures destined for immortality. Thus, a little later, when the Duchy was no longer more than a ruin, appeared the baroque cathedral of Brou the most beautiful image of flamboyant gothic in which, as Edgar Quinet has said, "was buried for ever the long dream of the Middle Ages."

This monumental splendor has scarcely been reflected in the eastern part of the

Duchy, which would later become Franche-Comté. The originality of the Franche-Comté country is that it long stayed outside of the French domain, into which it entered very much against its will when Louis XIV sent his soldiers there alrd put many ploughmen to the sword. From this it has kept an independant disposition, a fierce love for its traditions and a great mistrust for foreigners. More than any other province, FrancheComté, land inscribed in History and not at all defined by geography, unites countries very different from each other; but what binds them together is undoubtedly an identical relationship with work. What counts here is men's works, every-day works, patient, without fanfare, the humble mark of the human gesture. In the south and east, it's the domain of woodcutters, of woodworkers, and later of the artisans of clock-making; it's the tender, white universe of the fir-tree, from which houses and toys are also made. In the center, on the plateaus, men have become shepherds, and it is with the use of the pastures that they have become initiated to those rural collectivities which, from the Middle Ages right up to our time, represented one of the most fascinating forms of primitive communism. To the north and west, the Ognon and Saône valleys, separated by rocky plateaus formerly full of wolves, were lands of wheat, oats, barley and later potatoes. To the far north was the southern edge of the Vosges with its ox-drawn vehicles, its heavy farms covered with snow six months of the year, and its small factories born from ancient mines.

One should not look for the soul of this country in the city, but in the village, around the blacksmith, the dairyman, the harness-maker, and even the ironmaster. It was belatedly that the cities here became centers of commerce and culture. The world of trade is that of fairs and markets in towns which often had a precise calling: here horses, there cattle or tools. The world of knowledge was that of village churches, of little seminaries, of rural schools poorly kept up by people who believed more in the spoken word than in writing.

Of course, there is no lack of cities with a rich past and an engaging appearance: Saint-Claude, where the Jura Fathers, around the fourth century, pursued a mystical experiment comparable to that of the monks of Egypt, Besançon, where Vauban constructed one of the most beautiful urban complexes of the end of the seventeenth century, Dole whose University attracted in the sixteenth century the students of Poland and Spain. But the authentic inhabitant of Franche-Comté is beyond the walls of the cities, in the forests or the ploughed fields, except perhaps in that strange country of Montbéliard, long an independent principality and land of the Empire, crucible of a manufacturing imagination to which the industrial growth of the nineteenth century would give its true dimension.

Montbéliard serves as a bridge between Franche-Comté and Alsace, a passageway between the ploughman and the man of the city. Of course, Alsace has its vines and forests, its cornfields and its hops, but it's the cities which give their coloring to the whole province. They are so many landmarks on that route of the Rhine which was the great civilizing road of Europe. It is through these cities, small or large, but all equally coherent and orderly, that Alsace has been, since the early Middle Ages, the privileged crossroad of everything which the culture of our continent has elaborated in a fever or with patience. This old Germanic land has had from the beginning the calling of creating communication between two worlds whose distant gods and demons were not at all alike. This calling, which forms the basis of Alsace's trials, its conflicts and divisions, would also be the basis of its grandeur. It was because it participated in two horizons that it could reach that high point of inner tension which opens a whole people to art and works of art.

The creative fervor of Alsace was manifested from the Carolingian period, as witnessed by the admirable church of Ottmarsheim, was completed later in the Middle Ages with Le Haut Koenigsbourg, Murbach, Strasbourg. But it was in the fifteenth and sixteenth centuries, at the time when it sheltered the most pathetic voices of Rhenish mysticism, that Alsace was the great ferment of European culture: intellectual capital of the Germanic countries, it sheltered Gutenberg, Sebastian Brandt, it welcomed Erasmus and the young Durer in search of himself. On the Alsacian roads, those which lead to Switzerland, France and Germany, the myths and the new ideas, which would

drain humanism and the Reformation in their wake, found their final and dangerous form. The modern centuries haven't changed anything in this original destiny. Through much suffering, much heartbreak, Alsace has not ceased being, for the last thousand years, that imprecise and torn kingdom where the scars of History relate the long and necessary passion of the Mediterranean spirit and the gods of the inner lands.

At the heart of a triangle which would be roughly determined by the mouths of the Thames, the Seine and the Rhine, extends a vast territory of uncertain aspect: flat country, limestone plateaus, gullied forests, vast hills, a territory which only a long familiarity can make attractive. This heart is the heart of European civilization. On the shores of these lands, in the Rhineland and the Netherlands, in London and Ile-de-France was forged from century to century that Occident whose major vocation seems to have been to blend into a coherent architecture the ferments of the whole continent. The last of the Dukes of Burgundy, Charles the Bold, sovereign master of the rich lands of Flanders and Holland, prince of the blessed vines and the forests of his duchy and his county, dreamed only of one capital: Nancy, which he preferred to these magnificent cities, Brussels, Antwerp, Ghent, Lille or Diion, where the invention and labor of man had given to the art of living and the art of inhabiting privileges which time has not effaced. When, at the end of the year 1475, he entered the Lorraine city, he had the feeling of having finally found a history worthy of him. "Although the resistence had been long and obstinate", writes Michelet, "he granted the city the capitulation which it drew up itself. He submitted to taking the oath taken by the Dukes of Lorraine, and he received the oath of the Lorraine people; he rendered justice in person, as the Dukes had done, listening to everyone tirelessly, keeping the doors of his mansion open day and night, accessible at all hours. He did not want to be the conqueror, but the true Duke of Lorraine, accepted by the country which he himself was adopting. That beautiful plain of Nancy, that elegant and warlike city seemed to hlm to be, as much and more than Dijon, the natural center of the new empire of which the Netherlands, indocile and proud Flanders would no longer be more than an accessory." It was not simply a political calculation. Of course, Nancy represented the bond between the two separated regions of the Netherlands and Burgundy; but in the eyes of this sovereign haunted by mythical history, raised on legends and dreams, Lorraine symbolized that union of vanity and Germanism, of the southern and northern geniuses, which remains perhaps still today the only true driving force in the European movement. If we contemplate even hastily the destinies of these northern and eastern provinces of France, we can agree that the greatest part of European civilization has been accomplished on their fringes: to the north, it's the powerful communal impulse of Flanders and the extraordinary dynamism of the Batavian cities, the splendor of Bruges and Ghent and the fortune of Amsterdam and Rotterdam; to the east, it's Rhenish spirituality, the center of European philosophy, the marks of the romanticism of the night; to the south, Paris seems to enclose within its borders a light which makes the surrounding countries obscure; to the west, it's the spirit of navigation and adventure which would make of England, starting in the eighteenth century, the civilizing model of the whole universe.

But these centers of culture do not live in isolation, and the northern provinces are the roads on which they meet. This mediating vocation began when Charlemagne settled at Aix-la-Chapelle, it was reaffirmed in the twelfth and thirteenth centuries when Champagne became one of the most animated centers of Christian faith and of teaching. Gothic art found mysterious overtones here: not only in the great cathedrals of Reims, Troyes or Laon, but also in the multitude of little country-side sanctuaries which are in harmony with the infinite dimensions of the cultivated fields, the disorder of the forests, the green indolence of the rivers. In those medieval times, often troubled, to be sure, by famine, war or plague, a great activity reigned over all these countries. These were the most frequented roads of Europe: pilgrimage routes which lead from the Rhine to Auvergne and Compostella; commercial routes on which were found, frequenters of the fairs of Troyes, merchants from the Baltic and the Adriatic, weavers from Flanders and coopers from Burgundy; school routes also, on which clerics, half students, half vagabonds, went in search of a vague knowledge.

The particular originality of this country is the place occupied by the people in the cultural life. Whereas almost everywhere else, especially starting in the Renaissance, a very clear separation was made between cultured circles, the middle-class and the aristocracy, and popular circles, here the people, faithful to the medieval tradition, was not rejected, kept outside the living culture. Moreover, through its work, its dreams, its image of the world, it gave that culture its authentic density. We find the proof of this at the end of the sixteenth and the beginning of the seventeenth centuries in the multiplication at Troyes of editing and publishing shops and in the appearance of what would later be called the "Blue Library of Troyes." This library is the totality of those little books or almanacs printed on very cheap paper and covered with that blue paper which was used to wrap soap and candles and which we saw reappear at the end of the last century, at the dawn of lay and mandatory primary education, to cover the textbooks of little school-children. These little books were sold very cheaply by the peddlers or hawkers who, from village to village, from farm to hamlet, distributed a literature which is today singularly indicative of the popular mentality under the Old Regime. And it is at Troyes or at the many relay stations of Troyes publishing, in the cities and towns of the East and Center, that the peddlers came to renew their supply of books. Long forgotten, this popular literature is now coming to light, and in it we are discovering imaginary worlds in which French sensibility finds a formulation quite unheard of up to now.

But, more than the Blue Library, what best restores the true tonality of these eastern provinces is the painters of everyday reality, the masters of the silent life of the end of the seventeenth century, and among them, especially, the Le Nain brothers and Georges de La Tour. These were complete artisans who, no more than the illustrators of Versailles, weren't ignorant of the great laws of pictural composition. Thus, they were by no means naïve painters, intuitive amateurs inventing by artless plodding a world of depiction which is the very object of painting. And yet their craftmanship, their deep knowledge of pictoral resources are at no time separated from popular reality. They start from the land, the men and things of the land, trying to find, through the play of colors and shadows, the secret language of the peasants and the poor, the pieceworkers and the humiliated.

Here perhaps poverty finds all its nobility. At about the same time when Georges de La Tour was painting his Christmas Eve scenes, the village priest Meslier, atheist and revolutionary, humble minister of two parishes and harbinger of Babeuf and Marx, knew how to read this nobility in the oppressed existence of his parish members in the Ardennes. And in the name of this hidden nobility, he would show, in a "Testament" which is one of the great documents of materialist thought, how, since the Middle Ages , the people had been dispos s es s ed of its material and spiritual wealth, how it had been reduced to nothingness, by the upper middle-class and by the priests, in the depths of its spirit. As a matter of fact, the mystical religiosity of Georges de La Tour and the anarchistic atheism of the priest Meslier express the same love for the human condition, the same fascination for oppressed destinies, the same hope in that light which shines in the heart of the dispossessed. Neither one nor the other is a stranger to that smile of Reims which has watched over Champagne since the thirteenth century, no more than they are strangers to the tranquil oxen which, atop the tower of the Laon cathedral, watch the wheat ripen and the autumn woods turn yellow.

This permanence of the old popular heritage has not kept Champagne and Lorraine from being admirable cultural relay stations. Reims was already one in barbarian times, in the period when the builders of Saint Remi's Basilica were the educators of the whole Occident. Nancy was a brilliant one in the eighteenth century, at the time when the classical architectural model born in Ile-de-France imposed its rigorous arrangement, but also its perversions, on Germany and all the Slavic countries. This city then became a relay station for everything which France transmitted to the world and which could be seen reappearing at the Sans-Souci of Frederick II, the Saint Petersburg of Catherine the Great and the composite Vienna of Maria Theresa. It was a message from French artists to the men of the continent; and with the buildings, what France taught was an original view of happiness: conversation, romantic imagination, everyday comfort, a taste for luxury, a temperate philosophy of pleasure.

But these provinces, which have played in our history the role of an extremely porous filter through which Paris and France exchanged goods, ideas and sentiments with foreign lands, were also responsible, from the birth of our nation, for ensuring peace and order in the inner regions, and that is why so many successive misfortunes have come to be inscribed here, at the mercy of murderous times, for these were lands of invasion, carnage and division. What mysterious configuration has forever imposed on these places without contour, these soft hills, tranquil forests and vast fields devoted to wheat, the fate of being subjected to that terrible law of blood to which the nations have not ceased to appeal, making God the judge of their courage and their martial skill? However, the villages and unincorporated areas here have names just as pretty, as sweet as the hills of the Loire or the roads of the Rhone. Just in rereading the chroniclers of the Hundred Years War describing the burnings, the collective massacres, the destruction of forests or the extermination of flocks, we still wonder how human faces were able to come out of so many mists. And yet, since the fifteenth century, the forces of death here have not ceased to multiply. Those which emerged a little more than fifty years ago seem to resume all by themselves all the cruelty and absurdity contained in the bloody energies of the past. The angel of Hell has here unfold his fantastic wings enveloping in the shadow of eternity so many destinies brutally snatched from their peaceful march...

It is in the spring, in the exuberance of the vegetation, in the soft, slightly misty light in which the wheat grows green, that one should venture into these lands where the green tapestry of grass and trees has difficulty hiding the scars of History: Douaumont, Craonne, the Chemin des Dames, shredded signs of a sort of happiness suddenly blackened by fire and hate. Wherever the roads happen to go, repose the gardens of the dead, great cemeteries whose rigorous rows seem destined for the games of a childhood brutally torn from its innocence. These funereal gardens are now part of the landscape, just like the little village churches, the ancient streets of cities or the great sanctuaries of the medieval or Renaissance period. Everything here constitutes the inventory, without grandeur or beauty most of the time, of the immemorial effort of the human species tot survive the evil which is in it and around it. No where is the mysterious thread of that French genealogy, of that movement which from century to century binds me noneto another, more apparent. For, as Michelet wrote in 1842, "an intimate bond unites all ages. We, the successive generations, are held together not like the runners of whom Luvretius speaks, who pass the torch one to another. We are held together in a very different way. We were all in the loins of the early fathers, in the womb of the women of that time. An identical spirit runs from generation to generation. Instinctive impulses make us quiver for the past and for the future, reveal to us the profound identity of the human species."

These countries of the North and East demand of those who traverse them a particular, intimate effort to penetrate them. Here time has ravaged more than anywhere else the works of men, and yet it is here, perhaps, that these works have been the most tenacious, the most fruitful. Very little remains of the antique splendor of the medieval towns, of the Flemish festivities at the court of Burgundy, of the rich patrician dwellings whose contact with the Netherlands invited their owners to give a warm appearance to the interiors, to domestic existences and human exchanges; it is through the men that one must recover the riches of History, in the prodigious activity of the fields, the factories, the shops that one must grasp the energy of a people oppressed more than any other by the rigors of the centuries, but which nevertheless has not ceased to fecundate the French genius.

This energy can be found, but different, on the shores of the North Sea, from which somany captains, their eyes filled with dreams, so many sailors, intoxicated by the chimerical suns of the distant Tropics, set out on the open seas. Their epic has found neither its Daniel Defoe nor its Melville, as if the Anglo-Saxons had the privilege of giving form to those maritime mythologies to which the people of Calais, Boulogne and Dieppe are not at all strangers. But beyond their traveling vocation, these northern shores were especially cultural relay stations which played a considerable role in the formation of European civilization. It was here that the medieval routes for the evangelisation of England and the northern countries met; it was here that the great names of Christendom, Thomas Becket, Thomas Moore, Erasmus, passed by in order to give to their experience or knowledge their authentic universality. Calais is in the log-book of innumerable intellectuals who, from Canterbury to Louvain or Paris, went in search of their personal truth. The apparent rivalry which would long oppose France and England hid the true union of the English and Latin temperaments which was accomplished in these misty ports, under the restless sails of the ships of the frozen north.

Here geography explains the silence of History. The sea does not go deeply into the land, exerts little influence on the toils and worries of the inner country, which isn't the case, for example, in Holland, where through the configuration of waterway networks, the maritime spirit penetrates very deeply into into the interior of the country. Very quickly the sea is succeeded by the Paris landscape, that gentle sloping towards the basin of the Seine in the middle of which the capital was built. Before reaching the French metropolis, one crosses extremely diverse regions. This diversity comes from each country's relationship with the water, the vegetation and the nature of the soils, and it is found both to the north and south, the east and west of the capital.

*
* *

The closer you come to Paris, the more these landscapes appear like variations on a major theme, which is the city itself. This appropriation of the whole Ile-de-France by Paris is very ancient, as if there nature were a counterweight to urban crowding, as if the civilized beauty were the other side of all the ugliness, poisons and suffocation which a big city can accumulate. One can say that, from the twelfth century, when Paris stopped being a city in the middle of the woods and became the center of French life, this surrounding region, for a distance varying between twenty and sixty-five miles (30-100 km), has come under the aura of Parisian life: the country-side is the agreed place for being supplied with wheat, vegetables, animals for work and slaughter, but also wood and stone. Between Paris and its surrounding there is a constant movement back and forth of peasants, military men, but also of artists, builders; a sort of immense park is thus organized around its ramparts, pushed further back from century to century.

This park was first of all the site of lordly or princely edifices housing the intrigues, the loves or the exiles of the great men of the realm. Versailles would be the last and the proudest of these buildings, but Fontainebleau, Chantilly, Pierrefonds bear witness to the royal proportions of the architecture of Ile-de-France. More than any other, this country is that of the man on horse-back, not the man who us es the horse to cover vast distances as quickly as possible, but rather he who, according to what the day may bring, goes from village to village, from forest to forest, mixing a leisurely ride with amorous adventures or philosophical reflections. The major period of this region, close to Paris but so far from the clamor and the intrigues of the city, was the seventeenth and eighteenth centuries. The psychological novel and the philosophy of the Enlightenment were in a large measure the fruits of this landscape filled with urban mists, but which nevertheless keeps the charms of solitude. It was here that the Princess of Cleves came to light, that the meditations of La Rochefoucauld were born, and later those of Rousseau.

But it is here that the popular wisdom is expressed with the most freshness and savor. *Le Roman de Renart (Renard the Fox)*, human comedy of the medieval world, subtle parody of social disorders, sprang up here, with its grotesque or tragic world of the cunning, the innocent, the proud and the wicked. Renard is the man of the fields venturing into the city to capture its secrets without perishing by its evil spells. In the forests reign purer, whiter creatures: those which Gérard de Nerval would find, along with the girls of fire, in the hamlets of Valois: "Young girls were dancing in a circle on the grass, singing ancient airs transmitted by their mothers and in a French so naturally pure that one really had the feeling of living, in this old country of Valois where the heart of France has been beating for a thousand years." Here the forest and ist clearings are the domain of music.

It's at the edge of these forests, in that hollow towards which the winds and waters glide, that Paris is hidden. Paris is only incidentally the capital of France; it is wrong to see in it the happy union of the diverse national temperaments, to read in it a sort of endlessly moving summary of the whole country. Paris is a world apart, a miraculous secretion of History, to which no city of the past or present can be compared. This miracle remains deeply mysterious: the great metropolises of the world, from Rome to Brasilia, from Athens to Peking, have drawn their grandeur from a certain moment in civilization, have embodied in their splendor a certain movement of human destiny; Paris, however different its faces have been, embodies a thousand years of Mediterranean civilization, and the fascination which the city exerts on the whole world derives from a secret order which belongs without any doubt to the domain of the spirit, and her architecture gives to this order its flesh and warmth.

The brilliance of Paris and her singular constancy through the centuries, that constancy which means that still today the marks of medieval life are stamped in its streets and houses, are generally attributed to our kings, as if an identical thought had occupied their minds from the foundation of their domain. It would be more correct to say that Paris, mediating bond, powerful ferment of assimilation, hasn't ceased making the Parisians, and in turn, being made by them. More than the great, the humble count here, the people without a voice, obscure men, that populace, in a world, which in the most important moments has been the true heart of Paris. The true grandeur of the monarchy, and Henry IV is the best symbol of this, was, at least down to Louis XIV, to have chosen to live in the midst of this Parisian populace, to have accepted in advance its moods and its frenzies, to have never feared the innumerable excesses to which it let itself go, either under the weight of a misery too great, or because it had to express in a sometimes incoherent fashion a too great abundance of life, a need to conquer goods of which it felt it was deprived. The revolt of the butchers under Charles VI, the agitation of the beggars all throughout the fifteenth century, the follies of the Wars of Religion, the barricades of the Fronde, the processions of 1789 and the cries of the martyred of the Commune are so many backgrounds for the invention of Paris.

In this crucible where all the provinces have been mixed, where the foreign contribution has been constant, a world apart has been formed, which men coming from other countries contemplate with a surer gaze and which they call the World of Intelligence. To define this intelligence is a difficult task. Here is what the Count of Keyserling, surely one of the most lucid observers of the French reality, wrote about it in his "Spectral Analysis of Europe": "This city is a veritable phenomenon. Let's look first at its position with respect to France. This country has become in the course of the ages a unique social organism in this sense that it truly has a head, and only one, and that the rest of the country seems to exist only to nourish it. Of course, the French province has its own life, so much so that today the regionalist idea is again spreading. But its vitality is that of the stomach, the liver, the leg. However independent its own life may be, it never even considers ousting Paris; it is, on the contrary, precisely the depth and the force of this provincial spirit which garantees the persistence of the role of Paris. Paris is at the same time the brain and the solar plexus. Whoever has even a little talent aspires to go to Paris and goes there. And yet the meaning of Paris requires on the other hand that its determining stratum be reorganized hierarchically, always in a new way, with a constant exchange of elements. For Paris exists only by virtue of its purely qualitative attitude; the moment it no longer has this aristocratic character, it will be finished."

In rereading the innumerable chronicles which, from the Middle Ages to the present, have attempted to explain Paris, one is struck by the fact that, from its birth, this city has always been a revelation. And this should be understood in its double meaning and in an almost theological sense. Paris is a revelation for whoever penetrates it or for him who, having been born there, comes back to it after a long absence. There, neither time, nor seasons, nor beings are what they are elsewhere. At the times of the worst tyrannies, a subterranean freedom enriches the most modest aspects of daily life. Gestures and language acquire a new dimension there. There, as Stendhal pointed out, everything is always possible. But Paris is also that mirror in which each man can berevealedtohimself, can discover his true identity. Cruel, pitiless city, where the misery is greater, the solitude deeper, the vice more subtle than any where else. Rich and marvelous city, because in the disorder of the streets, the indifference of the crowds, the bitterness of the tasks, there are always those scattered smiles of old age or childhood, the softness of bodies and those spectacles of night or day which make of every passerby an actor, of all existence an ephemeral destiny, of all dreams an organized passion. For this city, well beyond its apparent unity, that which it gets from the buildings, the labors, the boulevards or the avenues, is made up of neighborhoods, and in each of these neighborhoods there are paths which only an ancient familiarity allows one to discover. And the genius of Paris is perhaps the fact that any human being can find his neighborhood there, that place in life which is the both necessary and ridiculous answer to his anguish, his concern, his joy.

IV

BOURGOGNE
FRANCHE-COMTÉ
ALSACE / LORRAINE
CHAMPAGNE
NORD / PICARDIE
ÎLE-DE-FRANCE

BURGUNDY
FRANCHE-COMTÉ
ALSACE / LORRAINE
CHAMPAGNE
NORTH / PICARDY
ÎLE-DE-FRANCE

BURGUND
FRANCHE-COMTÉ
ELSAß / LOTHRINGEN
CHAMPAGNE
NORDEN / PICARDIE
ÎLE-DE-FRANCE

NORD

Lille ■

■ Amiens

PICARDIE

Rouen ■

BASSE- ■ Caen HAUTE-

NORMANDIE

Châlons-
sur-Marne

Metz ■

Strasbourg

RÉGION
PARISIENNE

■ Paris

LORRAINE

BRETAGNE

Rennes ■

CHAMPAGNE

ALSACE

■ Orléans

FRANCHE-
COMTÉ

PAYS DE LA LOIRE

CENTRE

Dijon ■

■ Nantes

BOURGOGNE

Besançon

Poitiers ■

POITOU-
CHARENTES

Limoges

Clermont-
Ferrand

■

LIMOUSIN

Lyon ■

RHONE-ALPES

AUVERGNE

■ Bordeaux

AQUITAINE

MIDI-PYRÉNÉES

Montpellier

PROVENCE-
COTE D'AZUR

Toulouse ■

■ Marseille

LANGUEDOC

CORSE

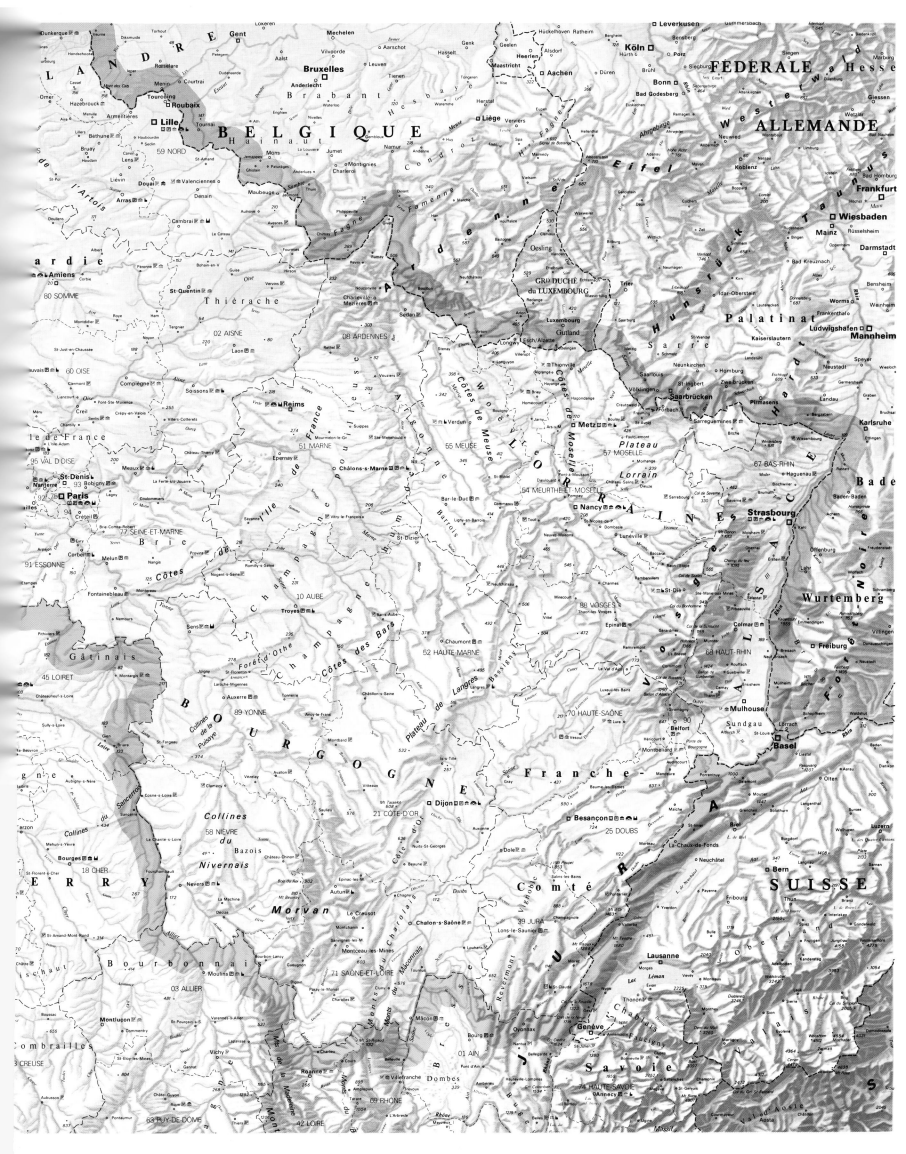

153/154/155

153-La basilique de la Madeleine à Vézelay
154-Paray-le-Monial. Intérieur de la basilique
155-Le perron du château de Saint-Fargeau

153-The church of the Madeleine in Vézelay
154-Paray-le-Monial. Interior of the church
155-Entrance to the château of Saint-Fargeau

153-Die Basilika de la Madeleine in Vezelay
154-Paray-le-Monial. Intérieur der Basilika
155-Die Freitreppe des Schloβes Saint-Fargeau

158-La cathédrale de Strasbourg
158-The cathedral of Strasbourg
158-Die Kathedrale von Strassburg

159-Les Ponts Couverts à Strasbourg

159-Covered bridges in Strasbourg

159-Die überdeckten Brücken in Strassburg

160/161

160-Le lac de Corbeaux dans les Vosges
161-Le vignoble à Ittersviller

160-Lake Corbeaux in the Vosges Mountains
161-The vineyard at Ittersviller

160-Der See von Corbeaux in den Vogesen
161-Der Weinberg in Ittersviller

162/163

162-Les grilles de la place Stanislas à Nancy
163-Les caves en Champagne

162-Gates to Stanislas Square in Nancy
163-Champagne cellars

162-Die Gittertore der Place Stanislas in Nancy
163-Die Weinkeller in der Champagne

175/176

175-La Marne
176-Le château de Chantilly

175-The Marne River
176-The château of Chantilly

175-La Marne
176-Das Schloß von Chantilly

177/178

177-La Seine à Château-Gaillard
178-La cathédrale d'Amiens

177-The Seine River at Château-Gaillard
178-The cathedral of Amiens

177-Die Seine in Château-Gaillard
178Die Kathedral von Amiens

179/180

179-Le château de Fontainebleau
180-Dans le parc de Versailles

179-The château of Fontainebleau
180-In the park of Versailles

179-Das Schloβ von Fontainebleau
180-Im Park von Versailles

181-Le bassin d'Apollon à Versailles

181-The Apollo Basin in Versailles

181-Das Apollobecken in Versailles

182-La Grande Arche de la Défense

182-The Grande Arche in La Défense (Paris)

182-La Grande Arche in der Défense, Paris

FRANCE a été réalisé
par les Éditions Hermé à Paris

Collection L'ALBUM
dirigée par Michel Laugel

Texte de Claude Mettra

Édition Bénédicte Baussan

Maquette de Michel Labarthe

Suivi technique CPE Conseil

Photogravure SNO

Papier demi-mat 170 g
des papeteries Garda

Impression CPE Conseil

Reliure SIRC

Diffusion Hermé

Achevé d'imprimer le 30 septembre 1996
pour le compte des Éditions Hermé à Paris
© 1996 by Éditions Hermé - Paris (France)
Imprimé en CEE
ISBN 2-86665-213-4 (Édition française)
      2-86665-217-7 (Édition anglaise)
      2-86665-218-5 (Édition allemande)